DATE DUE

Demco, Inc. 38-294

BEYOND FORGIVENESS

BEYOND FORGIVENESS

The Healing Touch of Church Discipline

DON BAKER

MULTNOMAH PRESS
PORTLAND, OREGON 97266

Cover design and photography by Paul Lewis
Edited by Larry R. Libby

BEYOND FORGIVENESS
© 1984 by Don Baker
Published by Multnomah Press
Portland, Oregon 97266

Printed in the United States of America

Library of Congress Cataloging in Publication Data

Baker, Don.
    Beyond forgiveness.

    1. Church discipline.   I. Title.
BV740.B3   1983   262.9'861   84-3417
ISBN 0-88070-054-8

    85   86   87   88   89   90   –   10   9   8   7   6   5   4   3   2

To the principal characters
in this book,
whose names have been obscured
but whose identity is well-known
to God and to me
and
without whose obedience
there would be no story.

Contents

Foreword — 9

1. Profile of a Sinning Saint — 11

2. What Do We Do Now? — 15

3. Confrontation and Confession — 21

4. Is Discipline Necessary? — 27

5. A Search for Answers — 33

6. Shaping a Course of Action — 43

7. Telling It to the Church — 51

8. The Church Responds — 61

9. Discipline without Destruction — 65

10. Forgiveness and Restoration — 73

11. Submission and Restoration — 77

12. Chastening and Restoration — 81

13. Set Apart to Serve—Again — 89

14. Restored! — 95

Bibliography — 99

Scripture Index — 101

Foreword

"Powerful. *Powerful.*"

I found myself saying those words aloud—even though I was alone. Tears of rejoicing filled my eyes as I turned the last page of Pastor Baker's vivid and transparent account of a sinning brother who had been forgiven—but much more than forgiven.

Here is an unforgettable portrait of biblical *restoration*, complete and victorious restoration.

Here, at last, is a living account of a local congregation who obeyed our Lord's instructions to maintain purity in the assembly—without sacrificing love.

Here is love that rises above simple, sweet sentimentalism . . . tough love, that finds its direction in Scripture and its resource in the Holy Spirit.

Here is the problem of sin, confronted by biblical discipline. The result? A brother restored to ministry, a family more deeply committed to each other, and a church body sobered and edified . . . sobered by the devastating subtlety of the enemy, but edified by a graphic demonstration that "greater is He who is in you than he who is in the world."

Here, surely, is an example of what the apostle Paul called forth from the Philippians: "And this I pray, that your love may abound still more and more in real knowledge and all discernment, so that you may approve the things that are excellent, in order to be sincere and blameless until the day of Christ" (Philippians 1:9-10).

Here, finally, is an undershepherd who took the instruction of the Chief Shepherd seriously—one who kept *watch* over the

9

souls in his charge. I can speak with more confidence about Pastor Baker's action than most who will read this account, because I count myself as a close personal friend. I have also been very much aware of the significant ministry of Greg, the restored brother, for over twenty years. I have watched the process as one who has a heart-interest in the outcome, and I am excited to the core of my being.

I am excited because I see in this real-life drama the potential for restoration, transformation, and yes, revival in churches across America: churches that are failing like Israel at Ai because they have not dealt with sin in the camp; churches divided asunder by discipline without love, discipline without restoration.

Yes—praise God!—it *is* possible to maintain love and purity in balance. Though you do not know the person involved in this true story, may God be pleased to allow you to enter it in such a way that you will find answers to challenges that you face. And may we all be drawn closer to the goal that God Himself set before us:

"You shall be holy, for I am holy" (1 Peter 1:16).

Dr. Earl Radmacher
President,
Western Conservative Baptist Seminary

CHAPTER ONE

Profile of a Sinning Saint

The silence of my study was interrupted by the persistent ringing of the telephone. A longtime friend from a distant city was calling. "I'm sorry, Don, but I have some bad news for you— one of your people has been deeply involved in sin for many years. The whole sordid story is just beginning to surface here, and I thought I'd call you so that you could deal with it before it comes to you secondhand."

I listened as he described a long series of events with all the confirming evidence that was needed. It was not just one of my people—it was one of my dear friends—it was one of my staff that had fallen.

When he finished, I replaced the phone, sat in stunned disbelief for a few moments, and then laid my head on my desk and cried.

Greg had been on our staff for two years—in the ministry for twenty-five. He was unusually gifted, affable, and quite successful. Everyone loved him. His sphere of ministry had captured the support and admiration of the entire church. He was relentless in his determination to succeed, terribly energetic, and one of the hardest-working men I had ever met.

We marveled at his creative ability and were impressed with his sensitivity. He was poised, versatile, and professional. He

11

displayed sincere humility and a willingness to please that was at times somewhat embarrassing.

We spent three months carefully considering Greg's résumé and past ministries before extending him a call to serve on Hinson's staff.

We thoroughly probed some hard questions:

Is he spiritual?
Is he emotionally mature?
Is he qualified to fill his role on staff?
Is he a team man?
Does he understand the difference between performance and ministry?
Does he have proven administrative ability?
Is he loyal?
What about his track record?
Has his ministry been blessed of God?

I called staff people and members of the three churches he had served. He had accumulated more than twenty years of blame-free ministry. Each contact that I made affirmed Greg's reputation for effective service and impeccable demeanor.

One deacon chairman in a former church characterized his five years with them as very successful. Greg had worked well with the senior pastor, and was described as dynamic and energetic and able to effectively motivate people to serve Jesus Christ.

I asked that deacon pointed questions about Greg's family life. "He has three really nice kids and a wonderful wife—they appear to have an extremely happy marriage," he answered. "He only left us because he wanted a full-time ministry. We really hated to see him go—in fact, we haven't had anyone since that has given us the ministry that he did."

Another church where he had served for ten years had only good memories of another successful term of ministry. The only negative comment was that "he worked too hard." "A real professional," they said. "We really miss him."

Greg had a heart for people—especially "hurting" people. He spent great blocks of time outside of his job description, working with students and with penitentiary inmates.

We have always placed high priority on the marriage relationships of our staff people. Joanna, his wife of more than twenty-eight years, was a beautiful, gifted, supportive woman. She appeared to be completely devoted to Greg. Her quietness never suggested to any of us that she was withdrawn or unhappy. It was just characteristic of a meek and quiet spirit.

Martha and I spent time with Greg and Joanna and sensed no tension whatever. Our first impression was very positive, with no hint of any reservations.

Greg was a handsome and charming man with a boyish grin that was oftentimes quite disarming.

He was a proud father, with three grown children—all of them "in Christ" and some of them in Christian ministry.

I loved to pray with him. Early every Sunday morning we'd gather in my office on our knees and commit ourselves and our ministries to our Heavenly Father. When he prayed, I always sensed depth and sincerity.

He had a delightful sense of humor and a graphic way of expressing himself. His crisp, descriptive speech left no doubt in anyone's mind as to just what was being said and what was meant.

Greg adapted to the staff quickly—but never completely. Our staff is confrontive and critical of itself and its ministry. We are always trying to improve. We spend a large portion of our time in staff meetings objectively analyzing performances, personalities, and programs, with the constant desire to perfect our ministries.

These sessions seemed to threaten Greg a little, and yet even that seemed to be nothing unusual. Confrontation is often threatening, especially to those of us who previously thought that "good feelings" were of greater value than "good performance."

Greg had difficulty separating his person from his program. Whenever any of us would question him, his tendency was to take it as a personal attack on his character.

But he did work awfully hard. Many times I encouraged him to slow his pace—take some time off—relax a little. Occasionally I watched him with concern and wondered to myself, "*Why this level of intensity? Why does this man seem so driven? Why does he perspire so profusely in front of an audience?*" I concluded that it was simply a very human characteristic of a very spiritual man.

We hug a lot at Hinson and often I'd reach up to this big man and give him a bear-hug before leaving our prayer meeting. This seemed to stun him. He often said he had never experienced that sort of a staff relationship before and that he felt terribly unworthy, but wonderfully accepted.

Greg turned down our first invitation to come to Hinson. He described a sensitive problem that existed between himself and members of his staff. His great desire was to remain, continue to address the problem, resolve it, and then, when that ministry was stabilized, he would consider leaving.

My reaction was that this was commendable. My failure was in not seeking out, in greater detail, more information. Had I called his pastor and asked for different points of view . . . Hinson might have been spared a potential tragedy.

So often, when calling a staff person, we feel an urgency so great that we neglect taking the time to seek out all the pertinent data. We virtually act like thieves, conspiring to "steal away" staff people from other churches, much as the competitive business world entices executives away from each other.

And so we called him, and eventually he came and he ministered. And he was greatly and deeply admired. I counted him as a dear brother and a close friend.

The ringing telephone and the faraway voice that early morning shattered more than stillness in my quiet office—much more. My brother, my friend, my colleague in the ministry was leading a double life—and had been for years. But now it was over, and his world was about to come crashing down.

So was ours.

CHAPTER TWO

What Do We Do Now?

What do we do? What do I do?

My first impulse was to call Greg into my office immediately and confront him with the information that I had just received. I'm so glad I didn't. I was hurt—I was angry—I was confused—and that certainly is no time to confront anyone. Especially one who has fallen so hard and so far.

I thought, I prayed, and then I picked up the phone and asked Pastor Dick, our staff counselor, to come up to my office.

I related all that I had learned to a stunned, disbelieving fellow servant. The whole story was preposterous. Impossible.

Dick and I sat there a long time. Grieving. Pondering our options. We knew some of our alternatives—but perhaps there were others.

We could ignore the problem and hope for it to go away.

We could pray and commit it to God and sidestep human responsibility by waiting for Him to take action.

We could quietly dismiss Greg.

We could publicly dismiss Greg.

We could ask him to submit a resignation and leave "for personal reasons."

We could blow the proverbial whistle on him and make it impossible for him to ever serve another church for the rest of his life.

All of these possibilities passed through our minds and tumbled over our lips as we stumbled blindly through a maze of confused and jumbled thoughts.

We finally concluded that some form of biblical disciplinary action seemed inevitable. But first we needed to confirm the story that we had just heard.

My friend had given me names and phone numbers to call. Two irate husbands, one of them Greg's close friend, were about to fly to Portland, confront Greg, and then visit with me. I called each one and listened as their deep hurt and anger spilled over the telephone. I listened as they detailed the incidents. One of them had since divorced his wife. Her "affair" with Greg was chiefly responsible.

I heard their threats. "This man has to be dealt with," they said. "This man needs to be disciplined—to be removed from the ministry, from the church, in order to protect the very people to whom he ministers."

It was at this moment in time, as I was taking concise notes of everything that was being said, that I coined a phrase—new to me—and scribbled on my notepad the words: *The primary purpose of discipline is restoration—not retribution."*

As Dick and I listened on different phones to the charges being made, we decided on an immediate course of action. We suggested to these two husbands that they remain at home and allow us the time to confront Greg with the information and wait for a response. If he denied the charges, then their presence would be a necessity—but if he admitted to these accusations, then we would be able to avoid what could be an extremely painful confrontation.

They both agreed to this.

Now, what do we do? Sufficient evidence to substantiate the charges had already been acquired, evidence that pointed again to the realization that some sort of disciplinary action needed to be taken.

I have always felt terribly clumsy walking through any experience of discipline—whether it be at home or in the church. My tendency has either been to overreact, oftentimes in anger, or to hesitate until any form of action has completely lost its meaning.

The biblical motive for discipline had always seemed somewhat unclear to me. Was discipline to be punitive, protective, corrective, or restorative—or was it to be all of these—or none of these—or was it to be one more than the others?

It has been extremely awkward for me to find the sensitive balance between the biblical demands for purity and the equally powerful biblical commands to love.

I thought back to a situation in a former church, remembering a scene in my office. A young husband sat beside me, tears streaming down his cheeks, and described his wife's alleged affair with another man. My responses were totally emotional.

I hurt deeply for my friend, and I feared greatly for my church. But I must admit that my fear for my church was greater than my hurt for my friend. I must admit further that my fear for my church was not so much for the weakening spiritual influences of hidden sin as it was for the limiting impact that unconfessed sin might have on my success as a pastor.

I attacked this suspected case of infidelity with great vigor, determined to preserve my congregation's purity. I confronted this young woman in the presence of her husband. I accused her without adequate proof. I warned her without any regard for the terribly deep and sensitive struggles going on within her. I demanded that she discontinue this unholy relationship and acknowledge her sin publicly or I would be forced to set the wheels in motion to put her out of the church.

Driven by my desire to preserve purity, I displayed little or no love. I succeeded in accomplishing very little—except that in warning the wife, I offended her husband, and the two of them forgot whatever infidelity did or did not actually exist and teamed up to oppose my pastoral leadership until the day I left that church.

I have also erred under the guise of love. Many times my sensitive nature has caused me to stop short in the terribly painful process of probing down to the deeply embedded roots of sin. I have put Band-Aids over festering sores rather than seek out the source of the infection—with equally disastrous results.

To display the love of God and the purity of God simultaneously is extremely difficult. Francis Schaeffer has said:

"If we show either of these without the other, we exhibit, not the character, but a caricature of God. . . .

"If we stress the love of God, without the holiness of God, it turns out only to be compromise. But if we stress the holiness of God without the love of God, we practice something that is hard and lacks beauty."[1]

Jesus displayed a beautiful blend of purity and love in His sensitive dealings with the woman caught in the act of adultery.[2] Without compromising the need for purity, He respected her personhood. The result was that her accusers' hypocrisy was substantially rebuked, the woman repented, sin was forgiven, and a sinner was restored to a place of dignity and wholeness with both her Lord and her community.

But what should *we* do?

Dick and I asked probing questions of each other:

"Is there any way that we can avoid public exposure of this sin?"

"Is it possible to keep this information from Greg's wife? His family?"

"Is it possible to keep Greg in his place of ministry?"

"Can he be restored completely without a resignation or without any public censure?"

"How can we publicly discipline a staff man without hurting the image of the entire church?"

"How can we begin lifting this man back onto his feet without crippling him further?"

"How can we protect him from his own weakness?"

"How can we preserve the integrity of the church and at the same time protect our members from any further act of immorality?"

"How can we be true to our Lord, and at the same time sensitive to the needs of our brother?"

Both Dick and I were convinced that whatever was done

---

1. Francis A. Schaeffer, *The Church Before the Watching World* (Downers Grove, Ill.: InterVarsity Press, 1971), p. 63.
2. John 8:1-11.

had to be done right. There was no room for error. Hinson's high level of visibility, Greg's popularity among the people, and our intense desire to see successful church discipline in action demanded that we proceed slowly and carefully.

We prayed, and as we prayed my own words came back to me—words I had spoken so often—words from an unknown source—words profoundly powerful—"*The church is the only army in the world that has the reputation for deserting its wounded.*"

Action had to be taken. Of this we were convinced. But as we ended our prayer time, we were also convinced of one other thing—we were not going to desert our wounded brother.

We did not exactly know how we were going to treat his deep and crippling wounds, nor were we sure that we could even save him. But we were not going to leave him on the battlefield, where he had fallen victim to our relentless enemy, to die or to only partially survive.

But first we had to confront Greg.

CHAPTER THREE

Confrontation and Confession

Dick and I were already seated as Greg came through the door. He was his usual jovial self. His inquiring eyes flashed back and forth from Dick to me. "What's up?" he asked.

At that moment I wanted desperately to trade my call to the ministry for any other profession. I wanted to be on any other planet but this one. I wished for someone else to assume my role as senior pastor, and then I wanted to fade into the woodwork and disappear. Oh, how I wanted to avoid the inevitable. But I could not.

"Greg," I said, "we've just had some very disturbing news. Dick and I have been on the phone all morning listening to acquaintances of yours describe you in a way that we have not known you. Two men have been telling us that you have been immoral with their wives. We have talked to the women, and they have confirmed the story. A pastor from the same community called and said that the word is out, and the stories are reaching scandalous proportions. Is any of this true?"

I watched him as the color drained from his face. His eyes lowered, and his shoulders sagged. I saw telltale beads of perspiration pop out across his forehead. He heaved one long agonizing sigh, shook his head, and said, "Yes, Pastor, it's true."

"Do you want to tell us about it?"

"There really isn't much to tell. They're telling you the truth—I am guilty."

"How long has this been going on?"

"A long time," he answered, head down. It appeared that all life had just been drained out of his frame. His body hung from the chair, limp and motionless.

"How long?" I asked again.

"For years."

"How many years?"

"Several."

"Two years?"

"Longer."

"Three?"

"Longer."

"Four?"

"Longer."

"Five?"

"Longer."

"Ten?"

"Thirteen, at least," he finally answered.

"That would be three churches then, wouldn't it?" I asked.

"Yes."

"How many women?"

"Several."

"How many?"

"More than I care to admit."

"Three?"

"No, more than that."

"Five?"

"Yes, five . . . no—six."

"Are you sure, Greg?"

"Seven."

"Any more?"

"Yes." He was groping, trying desperately hard to dodge the horrible, condemning truth. "*Ten.*"

"Any more?"

"No . . . ten women."

"Ten women in three churches over a period of thirteen years?"

"Yes."

"Were you a staff member in these churches at the time?"

"Yes."

"Who were these women? Were they church members?"

"Yes."

We purposely avoided any request for details.

"Greg . . . has there been any immorality here at Hinson in the two years you've been here?"

"No!" His answer was emphatic. "I came here determined that what I had done would never happen again, and it hasn't."

We sat in awkward silence for a long time. I really didn't know what to ask him next—and I felt restrained from further questioning.

As I was about to speak, Greg lifted his eyes slowly to me and said, "That's not true, Pastor. I have done it here, and I'm so ashamed and so sorry. The last thing in the world that I ever wanted to do was to hurt you or to hurt this church. I'm sorry, I'm sorry, I'm sorry."

I'll never forget the strange combination of deep sorrow and intense anger that I felt as I watched this wonderful man shrink in stature and bow in shame and weep in humiliation. Our working relationship had been destroyed. We had been defrauded. This man was as phony as could be and now there was a real possibility that all we had labored to accomplish could be shattered and destroyed.

I felt embarrassment. My credibility was damaged. I had been the one who had initially recommended Greg, pursued him, and strongly urged the staff and board to consider him.

I felt fear. I realized that the possibility for such sin lurked within all of us and later told Dick, "There, but for the grace of God, go I."

I felt empty. All of the great victories we had enjoyed and all of the grandiose plans we had laid were forgotten, and in their place loomed one stark fact—a bleak, startling, shaming fact—that completely stripped us of any reason to feel good.

I felt lonely. All decisions were going to be made only after collective counsel with the staff and board, but I knew that, in the final analysis, I would be forced to bear most of the responsibility for whatever followed. No matter what steps we now took, I would be the one to whom all would look for leadership. And if we failed, I would be the one to assume the blame.

"Does Joanna know about any of this, Greg?"

"No. I'm sure she doesn't."

"Does she suspect?"

"No."

"Does the family know?"

"No."

His eyes were desperate. *"Do they need to know?"*

"That's really not the question right now, is it, Greg? The question is, who will tell them? It's already public information, and it's impossible for this sort of thing to be kept quiet. They will know—and probably soon. I think, if possible, Greg, you should be the one to tell your wife."

"All right."

We made arrangements, the two of us, to go together that evening to tell Joanna.

"Do you want my resignation, Pastor?"

"No, Greg, I don't want your resignation—not yet anyway. I don't know what I want, Greg—I don't know what steps we'll take or which direction we'll go. We need some time to think and to pray and to study and to deliberate before we'll be able to make any decision."

"I'm truly sorry, Pastor," Greg said again—and again—and again.

I must admit that at that moment the words sounded terribly meaningless and empty.

As I stood up, both Dick and Greg stood. We moved toward each other, embraced each other in a desperate hug, and prayed and wept.

I drove Greg home that night. It was one of the longest trips I had ever taken. We were both silent except for occasional sighs and sobs that were called up from the depths of a grieving spirit.

How does a man tell his loving wife that he's been unfaithful to her—repeatedly—over a period of thirteen years? Not just any man, but a Christian man—a Christian minister—whose total life had been committed to sharing and displaying the holy nature of an impeccable God. A man whose position of trust had made such actions unthinkable—whose life had been used as a model for so many.

I was about to learn the answer to that question.

Joanna was a little startled to see me at the door at that hour.

Her apprehension noticeably grew as I told her that her husband was in my car and that we needed to talk where we could be alone and uninterrupted.

She and Greg climbed into the rear seat of my car and sat in stunned silence. Suddenly he broke into deep and convulsive sobs, took Joanna in his arms, buried his head in her shoulder, and said, "*I'm sorry, I'm sorry, I'm so sorry.*"

Joanna said nothing.

"I've been unfaithful to you," he finally managed to say. "Unfaithful. I've been living a lie—for thirteen years—with a number of women—I'm so sorry and so ashamed."

Joanna stiffened just momentarily and then without a word wrapped both arms tightly around her husband, drew him close to her, cradled him like a baby, and said, "I can forgive you, Greg—I love you, Greg, I love you, Greg, I love you."

It was hours before I left. Not much else was said. Not much else was needed. As I finally pulled away from that house, I felt anger again—but this time a fierce anger directed toward our mortal enemy, Satan, whose wiles and subtleties had again brought chaos out of beauty.

But I was relieved and surprised by Joanna's response to Greg's confession. It was far more conciliatory than I had expected, and if she were able to maintain this love and forgiveness through the dark days that lay ahead . . . maybe there was hope. Just a glimmer of hope that through it all God might receive glory, and one of His servants might be restored to a place of effectiveness once more.

It didn't seem possible, but maybe—just maybe—Greg could serve again.

CHAPTER FOUR

Is Discipline Necessary?

Some form of disciplinary action had to be taken. Greg's long-term sin was an offense to God, to the church, to his family, and to himself. And it was public knowledge—a major scandal in at least one of his former churches.

John Calvin, more than 300 years ago, reminded us,

> . . . if no society, indeed no house which has even a small family, can be kept in proper condition without discipline, it is much more necessary in the church, whose condition should be as ordered as possible. . . .[1]

That discipline was necessary was not the question. The form, the direction, the course of action, the short-term and long-range objectives were the questions before us.

Dick and I met with the other members of the staff and officers of the board and then repeated to them all that we had learned.

"One of our fellow staff members has engaged in repeated acts of immorality for a period of thirteen years—and with numerous women. He has had an immoral relationship here at

---

1. John Calvin, *Institutes*, Book IV, Chapter XII, Sec. 1.

Hinson. His wife is now aware of it. He has acknowledged it. This information is now public knowledge. What do we do?"

As I spoke, I watched each one as those shattering words sifted through their consciousness and then fell like huge hunks of lead into their souls. They were stunned—silent and sobered. Tears formed in the corners of many eyes. One man shook his head from side to side endlessly.

Finally a question penetrated the shocked silence.

"Are you sure that this is true?"

Dick carefully repeated the sources of information, concluding with the fact that Greg had already confessed to it all.

"Is it possible to keep this information from spreading any further?" another asked.

"It is already public information," I answered, "and offended husbands and wives are already demanding action. If we don't do something immediately, then I fear that some form of action will be forced upon us."

"What do we do?" asked another. "Any action we take could split the church."

This statement was an especially sensitive one. For nearly eight years we had been attempting to build an "Ephesians four" type of ministry at Hinson. We sought a ministry built upon lives patterned after our Lord's. We sought that visible oneness that makes the body of Christ attractive and irresistible to a world filled with separated and lonely people.

Greg had a tremendous "following" in the church. He was popular, effective, and well-liked. For two years I had honored him in private as well as in public. I had carefully and purposefully worked to see Greg accepted and successful in his staff role. And the sort of love relationship that this man had established with the people was one that could not be easily forsaken. People just do not fall in and out of love easily and quickly.

Discipline does have the potential of being terribly divisive.

As a youth I watched as an experience of discipline was imposed upon my home church with such shattering results that a state police officer was called to maintain order during one of our business meetings.

Our newest staff man had been on the job just one week. He was stunned when he heard me say, "Fellows, what we decide to do in the next few hours could cost us our jobs."

Another example—a recent one—flashed through my mind as I spoke . . . a church that had grown up on a restricted diet of love and acceptance. When the pastor of the church suggested a course of action against one of the elders that required some stiff discipline, the board came to the elder's defense. They fired the pastor.

Whatever decision we made had to be right—it had to be biblical. Not just for Greg's sake, but for ours, and the sake of the whole church.

Another staff person asked, "But who are *we* to judge? We have not sinned as Greg has, but none of us is perfect."

One man later asked, "How can we discipline Greg? He just did what all of us want to do, but don't for fear of getting caught."

I recoiled at that statement. Resented it. But as I reflected on what my brother was saying, I realized he wasn't admitting his own carnality as much as appraising the total untrustworthiness of human nature—the unpredictability of a deceitful heart.

The difference, however, is that though we are all sinners, sinning daily, yet we are also daily bringing those same sins into judgment,[2] acknowledging them, and experiencing forgiveness for them. If we were not doing this, then we would not be eligible to participate in an experience of church discipline, and we ourselves would be proper subjects for corrective action.

In Greg's case we were dealing with a persistent sin that had obviously not been forsaken, nor had there been any true repentance.

"Is it possible to help Greg find his way out of this sin without resorting to any public disclosure?" asked one.

To me, this has always been the ideal method of corrective church discipline. "Discipline behind closed doors," I call it. This is the sort of discipline Jesus used when He rebuked or corrected His disciples. A discipline done in private—away from the crowds—away from the trauma of embarrassment.

Oftentimes I hear the complaint that the church is not practicing church discipline any more. This is not true. We who are pastors, elders, deacons, church members are constantly rebuking, exhorting, encouraging, and warning our people—but mostly in private. Adjustments in living habits are being made

---

2. 1 Corinthians 11:31 and 1 John 1:9.

quietly without attracting public attention. This, to me, is the ideal method of discipline.

Jesus' loving restoration of Peter after his cowardly denial was hidden from prying eyes and listening ears. It was between Jesus and Peter. Peter was never required to make a public apology. He was not even commanded to return and correct his false statements to the young girl to whom he had lied. After appraising the awareness of Peter's own unpredictability, Jesus simply told him to go back to work.

Within the last few years one young Christian brother in our body was seen engaging in offensive, unchristian behavior. When this was reported to me, another staff person and I took him aside and lovingly confronted him. I told him what I had heard and then asked if it were true. He answered me that the charges were true. I then put my arm around his shoulder and asked, "How can we be of help to you?" With that his defenses sagged, and he began to weep. He accepted our offer to help, and his life has changed. This was an act of corrective discipline, done in private, and designed to correct improper behavior. And it was effective.

In 1 Corinthians 5:11, the apostle Paul lists six sins deserving of corrective discipline. Sins which, if practiced, actually deserved the sort of combined public church action that causes the sinner to be excluded from the church. "But actually, I wrote to you not to associate with any so-called brother if he should be an immoral person, or covetous, or an idolater, or a reviler, or a drunkard, or a swindler—not even to eat with such a one."

The sins listed here are certainly out of character for a Christian and need to be brought into judgment. That judgment can be personal and private. But when we refuse to judge our own sins as in the case of the arrogant sinner described in verses 1 and 2, the public action is required.

We are constantly taking private corrective action to deal with those who carry bad habits from the old life into the new, or when an experienced believer falls into one of Satan's snares. I prefer this method to all others and would have liked to have been able to quietly deal with Greg's sin in such a fashion. But Greg's sin was public—against the whole body of Christ. It was scandalous and destructive and required some sort of open and public rebuke.

"But this will destroy his family—probably break up a marriage," said another. "I'm not sure I want to accept that responsibility."

Again we were struck with the enormity of our responsibility. It was so important that each step be carefully measured and biblically right.

A divorce *was* a real possibility. And to see this wonderful family separated was a shattering prospect. Yet we had a responsibility to our Lord, to the Scriptures, and to our church family that demanded some sort of action. We had not caused the problem, and the possibility of saving this marriage was far more certain than if we allowed this immorality to continue.

"What if Greg decides to run—where does that leave us?" asked another. "We would have no jurisdiction over him in another church, would we?"

We agreed that this sort of response would complicate the disciplinary process, but biblical action still needed to be taken in order to (1) protect ourselves from any insidious inference Greg's departure might suggest; (2) protect any future church from the corrupting influence of sin; (3) protect Hinson from any form of compromise, and (4) protect Greg from himself.

Slowly, painfully, reluctantly, we all began to realize that we were on the brink of an extremely difficult public experience. We had no alternative but to protect the church and correct a brother, but there was a need to be fully aware of our biblical authority for whatever action we took. And we still had to determine the precise direction we would follow.

CHAPTER FIVE

A Search for Answers

As a shaken and grieving church staff we felt thrown back upon the Word of God. We needed a collective refresher course in the biblical teachings on church discipline, and we needed it immediately. Some significant facts became obvious as we reviewed the Scriptures.

Discipine in the church is not optional but mandatory— it is an absolute necessity if we are going to be obedient to the Scriptures.

Matthew 18:15-20 teaches that a sinning brother is to be (1) confronted, (2) reproved, and (3) excluded from the church if he refuses to repent.

Acts 5:1-11 illustrates (1) the seriousness of sin within the church, (2) the sensitivity of the Holy Spirit to sin, and (3) the quick judgment of God upon sin.

First Corinthians 5:1-5 teaches that in the event of persistent, unrepentant sin, the church is to (1) grieve, (2) deliberate, (3) judge the sin, and (4) exclude the unrepentant member.

First Thessalonians 5:14 commands us to warn the disobedient and the disorderly.

Second Thessalonians 3:6-15 teaches us to (1) warn the

undisciplined brother and (2) withdraw from him.
First Timothy 5:20 tells us to rebuke persistent sin publicly.
Titus 1:13 says to severely reprove those who teach untruth.
Titus 3:10 commands us to withdraw from one who causes divisions, but only after adequate warning.
Revelation 2 and 3 call the churches to repentance and warn of impending discipline if they refuse.

In these passages, God makes it clear that He intends the church to take corrective measures in the event its members persist in the practice of sin.

Whatever reluctance we as a staff felt regarding our responsibility to Greg, Hinson, and to ourselves, was cast aside in the light of these biblical admonitions.

Discipline in the church has many purposes.

To honor Christ
The practice of discipline is an act of obedience to all of the above-listed commands of Scripture.

To restore sinners
Matthew 18:15 states that the first consideration in discipline is that of "winning" or restoring the offending brother.
First Corinthians 5:5 teaches that even exclusion from the Body and deliverance over to Satan is designed to preserve the spirit.
Second Corinthians 2:8 commands restoration to the repentant sinner.
Galatians 6:1 urges the whole church to be actively engaged in the process of restoring a sinning believer.

Any form of discipline, whether it be a simple warning or the ultimate act of exclusion from membership, should always be understood as a part of the total process of restoration. The goal of discipline is not exclusion, but restoration.

To maintain purity
First Corinthians 5:6-8 states that sin adversely affects the entire church. Sin's presence permeates the whole Body. Purity is indispensable to power. The account of Achan's sin and the sub-

sequent defeat of Joshua's army at Ai[1] teaches the weakening influence sin has whenever its presence is allowed. For the years Greg was with us, a very subtle "feeling" prevailed. I sensed—somehow—that we had lost something. I couldn't put my finger on anything specific. And yet . . . the sharp edge of excitement was gone. The anticipation and expectancy seemed dulled. At times it felt that we were just going through the motions and that the spontaneous and the unexpected were missing. Many times I spoke to the staff and on one occasion to the board. "It feels as if one of us is living in a state of persistent, unconfessed sin," I kept saying. On the first Sunday morning after Greg's confession and the subsequent action that was taken, I sensed a marked change. I began to weep and turned to Dick on the platform with me and said, "God's back."

To discourage others from sinning

First Timothy 5:20 calls for a public rebuke of the elder who refuses to repent in order that others may fear the consequences of sin.

Discipline in the church is to be undertaken in a spirit of love and fear.

Galatians 6:1 exhorts us to be gentle and aware of our own humanness whenever we attempt to correct a sinning brother.

Second Thessalonians 3:15 warns us to keep in mind the relationship we have with the offender. He is not our enemy—he is our brother.

Jesus teaches the method of discipline.

Matthew 18:15-20 tells us how to perform the act of discipline. This passage is the first and the most complete instruction in New Testament Scripture on the subject of discipline. It is profound for its brevity and its thoroughness:

"And if your brother sins, go and reprove him in private; if he listens to you, you have won your brother.

---

1. Joshua 7:1-26.   • against you

But if he does not listen to you, take one or two more
with you, so that by the mouth of two or three witnesses every fact may be confirmed. And if he refuses
to listen to them, tell it to the church; and if he refuses
to listen even to the church, let him be to you as a Gentile and a tax-gatherer. Truly I say to you, whatever
you shall bind on earth shall be bound in heaven; and
whatever you loose on earth shall be loosed in heaven.
Again I say to you, that if two of you agree on earth
about anything that they may ask, it shall be done for
them by My Father who is in heaven. For where two or
three have gathered together in My name, there I am
in their midst."

The passage assumes relationship.

"If your *brother* . . ."

Church discipline is a family affair. *First Corinthians 5:10-11*
makes it clear that discipline is confined to those "in Christ" and
does not reach out beyond the boundaries of the church to the
world.

We had an established relationship with Greg; therefore we
had a biblical responsibility. Greg was not only a "brother," a fellow member, but he was a fellow servant. There was no question
regarding relationship.

The passage implies imperfection.

"If your brother *sins* . . ."

Sin is both a reality and a possibility in the believer's life. We
all wish it were not, but it is.

Our brother had broken the moral law of God,[2] had jeopar-
dized his marital relationship,[3] had offended the Holy Spirit of
God,[4] and had compromised the whole Body of Christ. Greg had
sinned repeatedly, and the impact of that sin had been felt in
every public service since his arrival.

---

2. Exodus 20:14.
3. Mark 10:1-9.
4. 1 Thessalonians 4:8.

The passage commands confrontation.
    ". . . go . . ."
    It is right here that most corrective relationships often break down. Confrontation, to many, is extremely difficult. To speak the truth in love[5] to an offending brother requires more than an insensitive accusation. More than a perfunctory rebuke. More than an unsubstantiated assumption. Confrontation, or the act of addressing the problem of sin in a brother's life, must be *pre-prayed, pre-thought,* and *pre-planned*. It must not be done impulsively or in anger since it is the first crucial and cautious step toward the restoration of a Christian brother. Since the instinctive human response to any suggestion of sin is denial, the first step in confrontation is critical.

    My first attempt at confrontation, years ago, was a disaster. I approached a brother about "a feeling I had," impulsively and in anger. He was at work. It was twenty-one years before I was able to approach that brother again, effect a reconciliation between ourselves and a restoration to God. Twenty-one years that were possibly wasted due to a clumsy, insensitive confrontation.

    One of my earliest successful experiences with confrontation occurred when I was the offender. It was early in my ministry. Four deacons had listened to my criticism of a fellow staff member and had been offended. They asked for an evening appointment in the privacy of my study. Their spokesman began with the gentleness of a loving father by saying, "Pastor Don, we have been listening to your criticism of Pastor ———. As you have criticized his leadership, we have all become quite concerned. We together feel that this is not right, that you're limiting the effectiveness of the ministry, and that this should stop."

    I had just been pummeled with a velvet-covered brick. Denial was out of the question since each one had listened to my complaints. Any attempt to justify my sin would have been futile. I knew that I had been wrong—I knew that when I was doing it.

    All I could say was "You're right, I have been critical, and I have been wrong. What would you like for me to do—resign?"

    "Heavens, no," the chairman answered. "That's the last

---

5. Ephesians 4:15

thing we want; we just want you to stop being critical of your fellow pastor."

With that the meeting ended. We prayed, each man embraced me, reassured me of his love, and left. I remained alone, wept, prayed, thanked God that my brief, inevitable encounter with a discipline committee was finally over, apologized to my fellow servant, and went back to work.

Three of those four men are still living and still ministering alongside me nearly twenty-five years later. I count them as treasured friends to this day. Their combined confrontation was impressive, biblical, and effective. It had been pre-prayed, pre-thought, and pre-planned.

Confrontation is similar to rescuing a drowning person. There is always the sense of extreme urgency, the carefully planned approach, calculated timing, loving firmness, and all of this with the full awareness of the extreme danger to one's own safety.

The passage commands reproof.

"... reprove him ..."

To expose and convince one of his sin is the meaning of the word *reprove* here in Matthew 18. Reproof is the gentle, loving word of warning that tells the offender that someone knows and cares about the sin in his life. It suggests that someone is willing to take the risks involved in confrontation and to spend the time necessary to help.

In our initial confrontation with Greg, reproof took the form of a question. After laying out the facts as we had learned them, our question to Greg was "Is this true?" A simple, straightforward, direct question calls for a similar answer. In contrast, questions such as "How could you have done such a thing?" place the offender on the defensive, cloud the issue, and often result in long and irrelevant discussions.

The first exposure of sin is as critical as the initial exposure of a wound. Great care is needed when the extent or severity is not known.

The passage demands privacy.

"... in private ..."

Christians oftentimes act scandalously here. Whether it's

pride or lack of self-restraint, I'm not sure, but so many of us seem to take delight in the weaknesses of others and take even greater delight in broadcasting all of the information at our disposal.

Confidentiality is crucial to the act of restoration. Many offending Christians have been discouraged in the process by realizing that their sin had become public information.

I learned quickly, as a father, that any form of correction accomplishes best results when done in private.

Sin scandalizes all of heaven. The fewer earth-people who know about it, the better.

The passage seeks restoration.

". . . if he listens to you, you have won your brother."

The goal of confrontation is restoration. There is a potential for great joy when a Christian obeys Christ's command to care enough to seek out the sinner—and to love that individual back into a vital, satisfying relationship with his Lord.

The passage teaches alternatives.

". . . but if he does not listen . . ."

The possibility of rejection, rationalization, attempts at justification, or even outright denial is always present. When any or all of these take place, then it's time to expand the sphere of information. Two or more witnesses are always required in Scripture before any accusation can be honored.[6] One witness is never sufficient.

Every time I talked with Greg, Dick was with me—not only for the sake of the biblical command for multiple witnesses, but also because my recall is not nearly as dependable as is Dick's. We would often ask permission to take brief notes of conversation. We never recorded any conversations on tape.

Two or three witnesses are not only needed to confirm the rejection of a reproof, but they are often needed to confirm the validity of an accusation. There have been times I was certain I was following a biblical course of action to correct a brother when I was actually mistaken about the charge—or lacked sufficient supportive evidence to continue. Other "witnesses" can oftentimes see sides of the issue to which I may be blinded. Also, the

---

6. 1 Timothy 5:19, Deuteronomy 19:15

accused may be more willing to respond to the other witness than to me.

If the brother has sinned, however, and if he persists in his sin, refuses to repent and seek forgiveness, then the added witnesses can confirm this to the larger body. They can also confirm that appropriate steps were taken and multiple warnings were given before more drastic measures are taken.

Verse 16 states that "every fact" or "every word" needs confirmation. When we are dealing with sin, we need to approach it with the thoroughness of a trial lawyer. We are not concerned with "hearsay" or "feelings" or "impressions." Even the words we use must be carefully chosen and thoroughly defined. It is so easy to get in a prolonged discussion in semantics when we're discussing sins. Words such as "adultery," "fornication," "perversion," "unruly," "disorderly," and "divisive" all mean different things to different people. Biblical definitions must be clear.

The passage expands the alternatives.

"And if he refuses to listen to them, tell it to the church . . ."

To the believer the church is always his supreme court here on earth—his final court of appeals. The church has access to greater wisdom than any human institution,[7] and the church always has a member of the Godhead present.[8] The church with its combined spiritual gifts, its limitless wisdom, and its God is capable of bringing combined pressure to bear on Satan that can limit his power in a believer's life.

One of our spiritual leaders, a woman, suddenly left her husband and family to go with an elder from another congregation. Their stated intention was for each to secure a divorce and then remarry.

The sphere of privacy was small at first—limited to just the family and myself. That sphere of privacy was expanded to the church staff and board, with the husband's permission, as the enormity of the pressure grew.

Staff representatives from both churches flew from Portland to reprove them both and to plead with them, but to no avail.

The sphere of information was expanded to groups within

---

7. 1 Corinthians 6:1-5
8. Matthew 18:20

the church as Sunday school classes, growth groups, and prayer groups were encouraged to pray and to write to this mother and express to her their love and concern and to appeal to her to repent and return.

At the end of three months they both returned and were restored.

The church is called upon to do more than expel or exclude in cases of unrepentant sinning. The church brings its combined power to bear through love and persistent prayer. Only as a last resort is action taken to expel.

It is obvious in Scripture that God always prefers repentance to judgment.[9] God is not indulgent, but He is long-suffering, and the church is called upon to display this grace also.[10]

Many times we would abort God's program of restoration by calling down premature judgment. James and John were ready to call down fire from heaven on the Samaritans for their refusal to receive Christ. It was necessary for them to be reminded that ". . . Christ did not come to destroy men's lives, but to save them."[11]

God is not indulgent, but He is long-suffering. Since the *Scriptures impose no time limit on sin or repentance*, we must be extremely sensitive to the Spirit's timing when it comes to the ultimate act of discipline.

The passage suggests the ultimate alternative.

". . . if he refuses to listen to the church, let him be as a Gentile and a tax-gatherer."

The painfully decisive step to exclude a brother—or a sister—from the fellowship of the church is sometimes a necessity. He is then to be regarded as an outsider. Gentiles were regarded as heathen. The Jew had no fellowship with them. The tax-gatherer was considered to be a person of low character who was obstinate, self-willed, totally unlike a child of God.

In other words, the sinning Christian is disowned as a brother and treated as a nonbeliever. This means he is excluded from the ministry, service, and fellowship at the Lord's Table. It

---

9. 2 Peter 3:9
10. Ephesians 4:2, Matthew 18:21-22
11. Luke 9:52-56

does not mean that he cannot attend the services of the church—even nonbelievers are granted this privilege. It is always well to remember how the church is instructed to treat the heathen . . . we send missionaries to them.

At the same time the persistent sinner is put back into the world, which is the domain of Satan.[12] The brother has chosen to serve Satan and is now relinquished from the protective grace of God so that Satan can do with him as he wishes.[13]

The final decision is made by a vote of the church or representative body, and that decision is binding. It is important that the action not be reversed until sufficient time has elapsed to confirm the genuineness of repentance.

The passage identifies the church's authority for such action.

> "Truly I say to you, whatever you shall bind on earth shall be bound in heaven; and whatever you loose on earth shall be loosed in heaven. Again I say to you, that if two of you agree on earth about anything that they may ask, it shall be done for them by My Father who is in heaven. For where two or three have gathered together in My name, there I am in their midst" (vv. 18-20).

The church, though comprising only two or three with the Lord in their midst, is qualified to discern the extent of sin to the point that they act as representatives of heaven in their decision, and heaven agrees with their conclusion.

But even as we reviewed the instructive passages some questions still remained. How were we to apply these passages to the specific case at hand? When should a person be disciplined? Who is a proper subject for discipline? What discipline needed to be imposed?

We still needed to know exactly what to do with Greg.

---

12. 1 Corinthians 5:5
13. 1 Corinthians 5:5

CHAPTER SIX

Shaping a Course of Action

Greg's sin was offensive to all, including himself. It had affected his ability to minister and had seriously disturbed and, in some instances, destroyed the relationships of others. But was it an offense that demanded total-church discipline?

The church's discipline of a sinning believer is somewhat like capital punishment for a criminal. It is the last—the ultimate—form of response that society has to offer.

We had to be certain, if we were going to impose discipline, that the sin warranted it and that his responses to our confrontation, which were all highly satisfactory, had not already removed the need for further action.

Offenses demanding discipline

Christians, although they aspire to be perfect and are commanded to be perfect . . . usually find themselves less than perfect. We all have blemishes and weaknesses that tend to tarnish conduct and deportment. These imperfections require encouragement, counsel, and kind admonitions and repentance—but do not fall under the category of demanding severe discipline.

Corrective church discipline is designed for sins of such a nature that they obscure the truth of God, bring into question the character of God, or obstruct the purposes of God.

Anything that endangers the purity, harmony, or efficiency of the church appears to be worthy of corrective discipline.

Doctrinal purity is to be maintained. Anyone who is guilty of rejecting fundamental truth or who teaches heresy is a candidate for church discipline.

Hymenaeus and Alexander were two Christians who fell into great error, saying that the resurrection had already taken place.[1] The apostle Paul called that sort of false teaching "gangrenous."[2] The sort of doctrinal poison that could cause death. Those who were guilty of pushing this damaging doctrine were excluded from the body and delivered over to Satan, that they might be taught not to blaspheme.

The doctrine of salvation by grace through faith deserves the utmost care in its preservation. In Galatians 5:12 the Apostle suggests some form of drastic action against those who would pervert God's grace.

In Revelation 2:14-15, the church at Pergamum is rebuked because they refused to expel those who held to the teaching of Balaam.

The doctrine of Christ is to be preserved at all costs. John tells us that the chief message of false prophets is that they deny the deity of Jesus Christ.[3]

At the same time we are to recognize the fact that due to culture, lack of spiritual maturity, and varying backgrounds, there will be any number of differences of opinion regarding teachings of lesser importance. We are called upon to receive the weak in faith[4] and not offend him with arguments. We are not to judge one another in meat or drink or in respect to holidays or holy days.[5]

Room for differences and room for growth need to be provided for a body of such diverse backgrounds, but no room for heresy can be tolerated.

The harmony and unity of the body is to be preserved. Unity is union made visible. The uninterrupted unity of the body

---

1. 1 Timothy 1:20
2. 2 Timothy 2:17
3. 1 John 4:1, 2, 3
4. Romans 14:1
5. Colossians 2:16

is constant testimony to the mystical union that exists between God the Father and God the Son,[6] and the unbreakable union that has been secured between the believer and Christ.[7] The church is the only place on earth where men can find peace—a peace that results from all the barriers between God and man or man and man having been torn down. In Romans 16:17, the Apostle urges the church to ". . . keep your eye on those who cause dissensions and hindrances contrary to the teaching which you learned, and turn away from them."

Sins of human character mar the image of the holiness of God. Moral impurity, perversion, covetousness, and idolatry[8] make it difficult to see God in the lives of His children. These sins are also pervasive and infectious and cause spiritual weakness to the body of Christ. The apostle Paul demands exclusion when these sins are not forsaken.

Any sin that is practiced without repentance, that obscures the truth of God by false teaching in an area of cardinal truth requires the discipline of the body.

Any sin that is practiced without repentance, that mars the holy character of God through unholy living requires discipline of the body.

Any sin that is practiced without repentance, that hinders the work of God by bringing confusion or division to the body, deserves—requires—the discipline of the body.

Who are the subjects of discipline? Are spiritual leaders subject to different forms of discipline than nonleaders? Since Greg was a member of the pastoral staff, was he above discipline? Is there ever a time when spiritual leaders are free to engage in acts of sin without the fear of discipline? Is there a difference between discipline and punishment?

The subjects of discipline

Any church discipline is grounded in the fact that God Himself disciplines His children. *All* of God's children can expect discipline ". . . for those whom the Lord loves He disciplines, and

---

6. John 17:21
7. John 17:23
8. 1 Corinthians 5:11

He scourges every son whom He receives."[9]

God disciplines directly and indirectly. God's direct discipline is often described as "punishment." The word "scourges" is used in Hebrews. The word implies that some form of pain is imposed upon the disobedient. That pain can be physical, psychological, or even material. The church is never called to impose punishment—that is God's province. The only form that institutional discipline or indirect discipline may take is that of reproof and then the final act of exclusion.

We could not punish Greg. What were we to do?

Since Greg was a leader in the church, we studied the biblical requirements for church leaders and the methods of discipline recommended when a leader sins.

There are many passages that relate particularly to leaders as over against church members at large; yet it appears that there are none which apply to the member at large which do not relate to the leadership.[10]

The following passages contain both a character reference for church leaders as well as the responsibilities they assume. Any church leader who fails in any of these areas would seem to be a candidate for some form of discipline.

The leader and his character

1. Above reproach (1 Timothy 3:2; Titus 1:6-7).
2. One-woman kind of man (1 Timothy 3:2; Titus 1:6)
3. Temperate (1 Timothy 3:2)
4. Prudent (sensible) (1 Timothy 3:2; Titus 1:8)
5. Respectable (1 Timothy 3:2)
6. Hospitable (1 Timothy 3:2; Titus 1:8)
7. Able to teach (1 Timothy 3:2; 2 Timothy 2:24)
8. Not addicted to wine (1 Timothy 3:3)
9. Not a fighter (1 Timothy 3:3; Titus 1:7)
10. Gentle (1 Timothy 3:3; 2 Timothy 2:24-25)
11. Not quarrelsome (1 Timothy 3:3; 2 Timothy 2:24)
12. Not covetous (1 Timothy 3:3)
13. Managing his own household well (1 Timothy 3:4)

---

9. Hebrews 12:6
10. Robert W. Cook, *Biblical Concepts of the Discipline of Church Leaders*, unpublished paper.

14. Not a new believer (1 Timothy 3:6)
15. Having a good reputation outside the church
    (1 Timothy 3:7)
16. Not resentful (2 Timothy 2:24)
17. Having obedient, believing children (Titus 1:6)
18. Not self-willed (Titus 1:7)
19. Not quick-tempered (Titus 1:7)
20. A lover of good (Titus 1:8)
21. Just (Titus 1:8)
22. Devout (Titus 1:8)
23. Self-controlled (Titus 1:8)

The leader and his responsibilities

1. To equip the saints (Ephesians 4:11-12)
2. To develop his spiritual gift (1 Timothy 4:14)
3. To lead well (1 Timothy 5:17)
4. To correct gently (2 Timothy 2:24-26)
5. To do the work of an evangelist (2 Timothy 4:5)
6. To hold fast the faithful word (Titus 1:9;
   2 Timothy 1:13, 14)
7. To shepherd God's flock willingly (1 Peter 5:2-3)

It would appear that any church leader who fails to meet God's expectations for one serving in the ministry—as listed above—would be a subject for discipline of some sort, even to the point of excluding him from his position of leadership.

As we examined these passages, we noted that Greg met most of the qualifications and ably performed most of the responsibilities.

The obvious areas of concern were found in 1 Timothy 3:2 and Titus 1:6, 7. Greg was no longer "above reproach"—no longer blameless. By his own actions, he had been disgraced and shamed. A blemish on his character had been exposed that caused him to lose credibility and confidence. Until that blemish was erased, his character would always be suspect.

Greg was no longer a "one-woman kind of man."

So often this passage is interpreted to refer to divorce and remarriage. The popular meaning is that no one who has been divorced and remarried is qualified for spiritual leadership.

The meaning, however, is amplified and the requirement

strengthened by a more literal rendering. "One-woman kind of man" means that it is possible for a leader never to have been divorced and still not be eligible. A man with a "roving eye" or a "flirtatious spirit" or even a man who lusts after or covets women other than his wife would be ineligible. Men who fantasize over other women are dangerous men to have in ministry because fantasy oftentimes becomes reality.

Greg was not only disgraced but obviously not completely devoted to just one woman. His immoral relationships with numerous women disqualified him for ministry. Other passages applied somewhat indirectly, but these in particular made discipline mandatory—a discipline that would necessitate some form of defrocking for this fellow servant.

We were convinced that action was necessary but in doubt still as to the course or extent of such action. For instance: Were we required now, by this passage in Matthew 18, to exclude Greg from our membership?

He had sinned publicly and persistently.

He had been exposed.

He had disqualified himself on at least two counts as a leader in the church.

He had acknowledged his sin, which may or may not imply that he was repentant. We could not tell if he was truly sorry for his sin or if he was just sorry that he had been caught.

He had confessed his sin to his family.

He was willing to do anything we suggested to him.

He wanted to be restored.

It also seemed that 1 Timothy 3:6 deserved consideration. Like a new believer, Greg needed time to reestablish himself in the church—time to prove himself. He had lost credibility in the church. His family's confidence in him had been shattered and he no longer had confidence in himself.

To relieve him of his position seemed proper, but to exclude him now from the membership seemed to be inappropriate. He had become a grieving brother[11] and to remove him from the source of comfort and strength found within the church family seemed to be filled with the danger of imposing a discipline that would be greater than he could bear.

---

11. 2 Corinthians 2:7

. . . so that on the contrary you should rather forgive
and comfort him, lest somehow such a one be overwhelmed by excessive sorrow (2 Corinthians 2:7).

How could he be restored to this body if he were not allowed to
remain in this body? And to whom would he be held accountable
if he left us?

Since Greg had disqualified himself for spiritual leadership,
he needed to be removed from ministry.

An overseer, then, must be above reproach, the husband of one wife, temperate, prudent, respectable,
hospitable, able to teach (1 Timothy 3:2).

. . . namely, if any man be above reproach, the husband of one wife, having children who believe, not accused of dissipation or rebellion. For the overseer
must be above reproach as God's steward, not self-
willed, not quick-tempered, not addicted to wine, not
pugnacious, not fond of sordid gain . . . (Titus 1:6-7).

This meant the surrender of his ordination. In this act he
would acknowledge that he was no longer officially recognized as
one duly authorized to perform acts of pastoral leadership.

Since he was extremely talented and always in great demand, we felt constrained to impose other restrictions. He was
not to perform any public ministry within the church, or outside
the church, without my permission or the permission of the pastoral staff. He was not to be allowed on the Hinson platform as a
leader or a participant without permission.

Since he accepted our reproof, we would not exclude him
from the church—in fact we would strongly recommend that he
remain in the church until such time as his restoration was complete.

"Thus it is not the will of your Father who is in heaven
that one of these little ones perish" (Matthew 18:14).

Since both he and Joanna needed help in understanding
and overcoming this problem, and since he needed the strong
spiritual support of men to whom he could become accountable,
we recommended that he receive professional counseling and
that he become a part of a supportive fellowship made up of men

who could regularly exhort and encourage him.

> And yet do not regard him as an enemy, but admonish
> him as a brother (2 Thessalonians 3:15).

Since he was a spiritual leader, and his influence was of such marked significance, we would require that he acknowledge his sin publicly to the entire congregation on the following Sunday evening.

> "Those who continue in sin, rebuke in the presence of
> all, so that the rest also may be fearful of sinning"
> (1 Timothy 5:20).

As we decided upon this course of action to be recommended to the board, it was with a sense of expectancy that we continued to pursue the matter. The fact that encouraged us was the complete and total submission of our brother Greg to every request imposed upon him.

CHAPTER SEVEN

Telling It
to the Church

It seemed that the whole city turned out that Sunday evening. Of course that's an exaggeration, for we couldn't even get the whole church in the auditorium at one time—but we were packed.

I had announced in both services that morning that, in addition to our study in Hebrews, chapter 6, that evening, we were going to be dealing with a matter of utmost urgency to the entire church family.

I said, "Tonight at the close of the evening service we're going to grapple with a problem that affects us all. It's very seldom that the church is called upon to collectively deal with the discipline of one of its members, but tonight we must do just that. Information has come to light this past week that seriously affects us all. It affects the spiritual life of every individual member. It affects the spiritual life of the entire body. One of our front-line soldiers has fallen victim to sin. Since Thursday the staff and board have met numerous times, and we have decided upon a course of action that includes the entire church. I urge you to pray much this afternoon that Satan will be bound, and that Jesus will emerge the obvious victor this evening. And I want you here also, with your family, that together we can address a serious problem and take the beginning steps toward correcting it."

And they came. In sharp contrast to the usual excitement that precedes an evening service, there was an atmosphere of sobered expectancy. It was unusually quiet. Many heads were bowed in prayer. The prelude was more reflective than usual, and I was terribly nervous.

This was not the first time that I had been forced to deal publicly with sin in the church, but this was by far the most serious and potentially disastrous problem I had ever faced.

It had only been two years since my leadership ability had been questioned in regard to another staff person who had resigned. I had been accused of orchestrating a resignation, being dictatorial and insensitive. There were those who questioned my decision at that time, and I was still smarting from some of the statements that had been made. The possibility that I could again be subject to attack was very real and terribly frightening.

I had spent the entire afternoon in prayer—sometimes alone and at other times with Martha or different members of the staff.

I had thought about the coming service, but had not written down the remarks that would be made. Instead, I brought to the platform some questions that needed to be addressed, statements that needed to be made, and an outline of biblical passages that would give credence to the steps that had been taken.

Many of us considered it providential that Hebrews 6:1-6 was the sermon text for the evening. I gave a number of varying interpretations of the passage and then concluded with an application that was appropriate for that evening.

I told my people that Hebrews 6:1-6 tells us it's time to grow up. Spiritual maturity is the stated goal of every believer. Maturity can never be enjoyed as long as we are forced to keep fighting the same battles over and over or as long as we persist in learning the same basic truths time and again. If we fail to go on with Jesus and fall back into the sin of unbelief or whatever sin continues to entangle us, we lose something—something special, something dear, something precious—and we lose it forever. Opportunities are lost, relationships are destroyed, people are offended, time is wasted, joy is dissipated. Any number of things are gone—some of them gone forever, never to be regained or restored. And we bring embarrassment to ourselves, our families, our church, and more especially to our Lord. Without my pre-planning or even truly realizing the appropriateness of my words, God used this passage to prepare hearts and minds for what was to follow.

Before closing the service, I announced that a special "family time" would follow the benediction. Visitors were welcome, but were free to leave if they wished. No one left.

Some questioned the fact that nonmembers were allowed to be present. We had discussed that problem previously and decided that since we were dealing with public information and since the outcome of the meeting would no doubt receive much public attention, then it would be to the advantage of everyone concerned for as many as possible to be exposed to what actually took place.

I called the chairman of the board and some members of the staff to the platform with me. After a brief prayer, I called Greg from his place in the auditorium to join me behind the pulpit.

I watched him as he reluctantly let go of Joanna's hand and moved slowly, apprehensively, up the steps of the platform. I saw his wife's bowed head, his son's troubled face, and I became very much aware of an awesome, expectant stillness that hovered over a disbelieving crowd.

As he approached me, I walked toward him, held out my arms, and hugged him tightly. We both wept. I could feel the tension in his body and could hear the sobs that stirred from somewhere deep within him.

After regaining my composure somewhat, I stood before my people in silence, looking from one side of that auditorium to the other, sighed deeply, and looked at Greg and said, "I missed you on the platform with me today, Greg. It just didn't seem right—in fact it seemed terribly wrong. You belong here, and when you're missing, I feel that the team has lost a great deal of its punch and its effectiveness."

His face, red and heavy with perspiration, was bowed.

"Yes," he said softly.

I turned to the congregation. "There have been things brought to our attention this week," I said, "that tell us that one of the members of the team—one of our soldiers—has fallen in battle. One of our warriors is down. He needs tonight to have an opportunity to bare his heart to the family. He needs also to feel the love and forgiveness of his church family. We, the staff and board, with his and Joanna's consent, have asked him to share what's in his life."

With that brief introduction, Greg stepped up and began to speak. His voice was weak and hoarse from crying. His shoulders sagged, and he held the sides of the pulpit for support. Never did he lift his eyes to see the faces that were intently watching his every move.

"I stand before you as an example of what Pastor was preaching about tonight," Greg said. "I stand here to ask your forgiveness for inexcusable behavior. I have resigned, I am surrendering my ordination, because I have been unfaithful to my wife, here and in two prior churches—not just once but many times, and with many different women. When I came to Hinson, I felt that I had left this sin behind me, but I hadn't. Would to God I could start over again, but as Pastor said, 'You can't. Something has been lost.' I've lost something. I have hurt innocent people. I've hurt you, I've hurt Pastor, because I came here under false pretenses. I frankly duped all of you into believing that I was something that I was not.

"I beg your forgiveness—I plead for it—and I do pray that if any of you are considering some similar course of action, that you will see what it's costing and turn away from it and allow God to cleanse you. I believe He has cleansed me, but the scars will always remain.

"My beautiful wife has forgiven me and has consented to continue living with me, and I don't know how I can ever thank her for that—"

Greg lost control of himself at this point and sobbed openly before the people. I felt clumsy for him. I wanted to stand and help him, to support him, to strengthen him, but, no, this was not the moment for me to interfere with the sacred act of confession. The deep, deep struggles that ensue when sin and repentance lock themselves together in a struggle to the death must be allowed to continue. Sin must be destroyed—it cannot be comforted.

After what appeared to be hours—but in reality were just brief, but agonizing, moments, Greg continued.

"In these coming days I would appreciate your prayers that I will continue to grow. I've started, and I'm not growing simply because I've been caught; I'm now growing because I want to.

"I am glad I was caught—and what a beautiful sense of timing God has to let it happen tonight when Pastor was preaching on Hebrews, chapter 6.

"So please forgive me and pray for us. We have some rocky days ahead—all of which I deserve, but not my family."

The congregation was silent, intently interested, but totally silent. No one moved, no one spoke, no one even coughed. Some heads were bowed, many eyes were moist, but no one seemed to quite know what to do next. It was obvious that Greg's words had gripped hearts firmly and deeply and that many were troubled. Some undoubtedly were feeling the fear that comes with another's exposure.

I asked Greg to be seated with Joanna and then said, "I want to speak to the family for just a few minutes from the Scriptures. I told Greg Thursday that no matter what happened, I loved him and would continue to love him. I told him, too, that as surprising as it may seem, I have a hunch that this church family is going to continue to love him, too.

"What we have done tonight," I said, "I hope only has to be done once—for all time. I hope this never happens again. Some of you, I'm sure, are thinking: 'IS THIS PROBLEM SO SERIOUS AS TO REQUIRE THIS SORT OF A MEETING?' "

With that question in mind I encouraged the people to turn with me to 1 Corinthians, chapter 5. "In this passage, we have the account of a church member who was living in continued, unrepentant, moral sin. He was arrogant. The church was tolerant, and the Apostle was insistent that the problem was of such magnitude that it required immediate, public, corrective action.

"Contrary to what we are seeing tonight, the Corinthian believer, along with other church members, was unconcerned and unrepentant. Greg is not displaying arrogance . . . and we are not displaying lack of concern.

"In Corinth, however, there seemed to be something resembling pride over this sin—a sin that was growing to scandalous proportions in the community. Here are some of the things this passage relates about the situation.

'It is actually reported that there is immorality among you . . .' (v. 1).

It was public information.

'. . . and immorality of such a kind as does not exist even among the Gentiles, that someone has his father's wife . . .' (v. 1).

It was a sin uncommon even among the heathen.

'And you have become arrogant, and have not mourned instead . . .' (v. 2).

It was being ignored and tolerated.

. . . in order that the one who had done this deed might be removed from your midst' (v. 2).

It required, instead, the exclusion of the sinner.

'For I, on my part, though absent in body but present in spirit, have already judged him who has so committed this, as though I were present. In the name of our Lord Jesus, when you are assembled, and I with you in spirit, with the power of our Lord Jesus . . .' (vv. 3-4).

It demanded the assembled action of the congregation.

'I have decided to deliver such a one to Satan for the destruction of his flesh, that his spirit may be saved in the day of the Lord Jesus' (v. 5).

It presumed the need for the ultimate discipline.

'Your boasting is not good. Do you not know that a little leaven leavens the whole lump of dough?' (v. 6).

If undisciplined, it could infect the whole body.

'Clean out the old leaven, that you may be a new lump, just as you are in fact unleavened. For Christ our Passover also has been sacrificed' (v. 7).

The sacrifice of Christ for sin demands the judgment of sin.

"The passage continues to list other sins that require similar action by the church body if they are permitted to continue. The list not only includes sins of moral impurity, but expands to embrace covetousness or lust, reviling or abusive speech, drunkenness, swindling, or cheating.

"Is the problem so serious, you ask? This passage declares

that all sin is serious because all sin caused the death of Christ, shames the body, and infects the church if it is not properly addressed.

"There is a second question some of you may be asking: WHY ARE WE DOING IT SO PUBLICLY? SHOULDN'T THIS BE DONE PRIVATELY? WHY IS IT NECESSARY TO EXPOSE THIS DEAR BROTHER TO SUCH PUBLIC EMBARRASSMENT?

"It's very seldom that we engage in discipline in such a public way. Most discipline that goes on here is done in private. You never know about it, and I'm convinced that that is the way it should be done.

"There are three reasons for taking such drastic measures:

"One, the nature of the sin and its persistence demands radical attention. An ongoing moral sin that has continued for thirteen years and damaged many lives will probably not be forsaken without such attention as we are giving it tonight.

"Two, the sin is public information and requires public action.

"Three, and finally, because the Scriptures tell us to do it this way. First Timothy, chapter 5, verses 17 to 22, talks about church leaders—how they should be honored and how they should be rebuked. Verse 19 says, 'Do not receive an accusation against an elder except on the basis of two or three witnesses.'

"As we began receiving and making phone calls last Thursday, and as I became aware of the nature of those calls, I asked Pastor Dick to join me on his phone line and together we listened to every complaint and every accusation. Together we questioned every statement until we were mutually satisfied that we both had heard, understood, and believed what was being said.

"Verse 20 states, 'Those who continue in sin, rebuke in the presence of all, so that the rest also may be fearful of sinning.'

"Public servants, like those of us in leadership in the church, deserve public rebuke whenever we break a public trust. That is why we have reluctantly gone so public tonight. We want you to follow our example when it is worth following, but when it is not, we want you to be warned so as to not make the same mistake we have.

"The most difficult thing for those of us in spiritual leadership to do is to publicly expose personal sin in this way. It's difficult enough for us to deal with our own private sins.

"The apostle Paul warns us in 1 Corinthians 11:27-30 that failure to bring sin into judgment can cause weakness, sickness, and death. He reemphasizes his statement in verse 32 when he states that refusal to judge our sins results in the chastisement of God.

"I dislike what I am doing tonight—intensely—but I dislike the alternative even more. The dissension and distrust that this problem would create if it were handled any other way could be disastrous. There is more sin lying under the proverbial rug than the rug can cover and far more than the church can handle.

"Another question you might be asking is WHAT DO WE DO NOW?

"Turn again in your Bible to 2 Corinthians, chapter 2. We have been told what to do in the event of persistent sin and in the event that the sinner is a leader in the church. What do we do now that he has asked forgiveness?

"Chapter 2, verses 1 to 11 tell us how and why to restore a repentant brother in Christ. This passage is speaking directly of the immoral person in 1 Corinthians, chapter 5, but indirectly of Greg. Greg meets the qualifications for such a response from us tonight.

> Sufficient for such a one is this punishment which was inflicted by the majority, so that on the contrary you should rather forgive and comfort him, lest somehow such a one be overwhelmed by excessive sorrow (vv. 6-7).

"Since confession in this instance was complete, forgiveness was in order.

"Greg's confession has also been complete. He has bared his heart to every member of his immediate family and to others. He has called those whom he sinned against and asked their forgiveness. Tonight he has asked our forgiveness, and we must forgive him.

"Another question is probably in many minds now: IF WE ARE FORGIVING HIM AND RESTORING HIM, WHY CAN'T HE CONTINUE IN HIS PRESENT MINISTRY?

"Greg has been wounded, critically wounded, and the wounded need time for wounds to heal. Greg has been emotionally, spiritually, physically wounded. He is embarrassed, ashamed, terribly depressed, and he needs time to recover.

"He needs to rebuild confidence in himself, and we need time to rebuild our confidence in him. He needs to be proven, and such proving will take time.

"In order to help him reestablish himself, we have made certain recommendations to him—to which he has already agreed, and some of which he has already performed.

"One, that he acknowledge his sin to his wife and family.

"Two, that he confess his sin to the church family.

"Three, that he surrender his ordination until such a time that we feel he might again be qualified for ministry.

"Four, that he not engage in any public ministry without our permission.

"Five, that he submit to extensive psychological counseling. We recommended a psychologist within the church family, and offered to pay counseling fees if necessary.

"Six, that he and his family remain right here in Hinson and allow us the privilege of helping in his restoration.

"We have asked his family to remain in their places of present ministry. They can't believe that we would accept them after what has happened, but I'm convinced that the church is a redemptive society—not only for those on the outside, but those on the inside as well.

"We have encouraged Greg to seek secular employment. Whether there are jobs available I don't know, but I wouldn't be surprised if someone here tonight knew of something.

"We are going to pray for Greg, that he will be empowered by God to break a pattern that has existed for thirteen years, and that he will be restored fully to a ministry that is productive and fruitful.

"How long will it take? I don't know. But a sufficient length of time to prove to himself, to his family, to his church family, and to his God that he is truly spiritually mature enough to carry on a ministry where he can honor Christ.

"So we've asked him to stay right here and be restored.

"It's been said of the family of God that it's the only army in the world that deserts its wounded. One of our family has been wounded, but by God's grace, we are not going to desert him, do you agree?"

I was not prepared for the response that followed. The entire congregation stood to its feet and applauded—a long-sustained, overwhelming applause that caused me and Greg and Joanna and most everyone else in the building to collapse in tears.

Before leaving and after prayer, I said, "I want to ask one more thing of the church. It has all been said. There's no need to say more. All the questions have been answered. There's no reason to ask any more. Nothing stops the rumor mill faster than when it's all been said. Now, let's talk to God and reclaim our brother to complete and total restoration—and let's go home."

But they did not go home. For two hours the church family stood in a single line so that each could embrace and encourage Greg and Joanna and pledge their support in the difficult months that lay ahead.

CHAPTER EIGHT

The Church Responds

As I left the church that night, I felt drained—emotionally, physically, spiritually—and terribly lonely. The incidents recorded so far had consumed nearly every moment of the past eighty-three hours. From the first phone call, to the confrontation, to the staff and board discussions, and on to the general meeting of the church, we had consumed more than three full days.

My mind had thought of little else since the moment of the first phone call. And now it was over. Or at least—we had ended the beginning. There would be much that followed, of course, but the initial trauma was past. The church had been told, and the response to it all seemed generally favorable.

Martha and I sat silently at home that night, wondering what the other was thinking and possibly wondering even more what we ourselves were thinking. We were both uncertain. Did we do the right thing—take the right action—say the right words? Did we display a proper balance between love and purity? Were we too loving to the point of condoning . . . or too demanding to the point of damaging?

We needed approval so desperately, yet who was to approve? The whole church family was focusing all of its concern on the one who really needed that concern—the one whose obvious pain had captured their attention and sympathy.

I think for a few brief moments I better understood the prodigal son's elder brother in Luke's Gospel, chapter 15. He had felt that sin was receiving a greater reward than righteousness. All of the joy and the merriment that came with his brother's repentance overwhelmed him, and he felt the disturbing pangs of resentment and jealousy. I must confess that I wondered at the outpourings of love that were being made in response to the insidious sin that had been confessed.

But then the values of heaven came back into focus. Martha and I began to realize that the response of our people to Greg's confession was similar to what was actually taking place in the presence of God, for ". . . there is joy in the presence of the angels of God over one sinner who repents."[1]

The only thing left for us was the thing we needed the most—a moment of thanksgiving and a night of sleep.

The reactions were quick in coming. Telephone calls, letters, notes, personal words. Most of them encouraging.

One member wrote:

The restoration service was beautiful and fitting. If my husband had been *discovered*, forgiven, and restored by the church, perhaps he would still be alive today. I believe the Lord may have taken him while his testimony still looked good to those around him.

Another said:

Thank you for your obedience to the Word of God in the area of church discipline. . . .

And another:

I have been terribly hurt by what has happened recently, but I have grown spiritually through it all.

A letter stated:

Your handling of the exposure of sin in Christian conduct by a member of the Hinson staff was my first experience with a church involved in a disciplinary action.

---

1. Luke 15:10

You proved that this task can be handled without malice or revenge to the extent that the offender might be reclaimed and restored to fellowship.

A seminary professor said:

At last I think I have seen it done right . . .

Of the numerous notes and letters that came to my desk, the one that meant the most came from Greg himself:

Dear Pastor,

Joanna and I wish to thank you for the key part you played in my confrontation, confession, and restoration. There are no words which could adequately express our love and gratitude for your wisdom and willingness to be used of God in our healing.

I still grieve at the hurt done to the body at Hinson, even though we see God working to cause my foolishness to glorify Himself.

Thank you for suggesting that we stay in the Body. . . . We plan to remain. It looks as if there might be a possibility of employment with an insurance company as agent. We are doing our best to be sensitive to God's leading.

We are also seeing growth in my leadership, spiritually, in the home. Joanna is seeing the man of God emerge that she has always craved. I pray God that I'll not fail her again in this area or any other.

Again, all our family stands forever in your debt because you dared to do what was right even though it was never easy.

We love you deeply.

Sincerely,

Greg & Joanna

Yet there were those who disapproved—and that was their

right and their privilege.

Some felt that in parading sin so publicly, we had glorified it.

Others felt that we had been too easy on Greg and that our young people would not have the proper attitude toward the destructive nature of sin because we had forgiven it so easily.

There were those who were angry—terribly angry—over the deception that Greg had thrust upon them.

Many felt that removing Greg from his position of leadership was not justified since he had confessed his sin publicly and evidently forsaken it.

One letter read:

I personally feel that removing Greg from spiritual leadership is a travesty on the grace of a forgiving God. You require more pounds of flesh than does God Himself. What more must a person do to prove his sincerity?

Many wrote letters expressing their great concern that regardless of however long it took, Greg should be restored to his place of ministry. They felt strongly that restoration, if it was to be complete, meant that he again be given the full responsibilities and privileges of ministry here at Hinson.

It's always flattering to pastor a congregation that feels the freedom to express their minds. But it is also disconcerting and oftentimes terribly confusing. It was obvious that we could not please everyone. It was also characteristic of my humanness to be more devastated by one criticism than encouraged by one hundred letters of praise.

As a staff we considered all the comments and were moved again back to the one position of safety and satisfaction. Our concern had to be for the full approval of only One—our Lord—and we prayed that time would confirm that we had taken a Christ-honoring position that would ultimately glorify Him and Him alone.

CHAPTER NINE

Discipline without Destruction

How does a church discipline a brother without destroying him? How does a family of believers express disgust for sin without displaying disdain to the believer? How can a man be set aside and yet still maintain some semblance of hope? What tools can be employed that might possibly hasten restoration? What mistakes did I make that slowed the process? Those were questions which came to my mind again and again during those trying months of discipline.

The most difficult and yet the most crucial decision that we had made was to request Greg and Joanna to remain at Hinson Church. We didn't realize at the time what a big part this was to play in the restoration process.

The threat of discipline usually results in departure. Most disciplined church members leave their church or are asked to leave. When this happens, however, the problem is rarely corrected. It is simply transplanted.

Exclusion or withdrawal does not imply departure. The rights and privileges that are withdrawn are meant to cause sorrow and shame to the point of repentance, and such repentance is meant to lead to requests for forgiveness and restoration to the excluding body.

The large number of churches available to the average

Christian today make discipline and restoration difficult. It becomes a fairly simple matter for a sinning member to quickly lose himself in another congregation and then soon forget or cover over the real reason that forced him to change churches.

When spiritual leaders fall in sin, the first concern is to remove them quickly and as far away as possible. This accomplishes nothing. The sinner is uncorrected, and the church is denied the opportunity to learn vital lessons about sin, forgiveness, and restoration.

The church is notoriously weak in disciplining its sinning pastors. Pastors are human, have weaknesses, and fall in sin just like other church members.

Recently a prominent pastor was discovered in a compromising situation that suggested moral impurity. He was confronted. He admitted to indiscretion but refused to accept any responsibility for his actions. He was asked to resign. He left guilty, but he left behind him a totally bewildered church family whose feelings ranged from anger to guilt. He assumed a pastorate in another church and soon revealed again that he was morally irresponsible. That man has had five short-term pastorates in as many years, and has been forced to leave each one for reasons of moral impurity. His departures were not disciplinary in nature. The church just got rid of its problem. He was able to transfer his problem to another unsuspecting congregation.

Discipline demands accountability, and effective accountability is impossible among strangers.

One of the many mistakes I made during Greg's twenty-six-month restoration period was that I failed to maintain constant contact with him. In fact, Greg admitted later that he felt that I and other members of the staff had let him down. One staff person took him to lunch . . . once. I met with him occasionally and called periodically, but we never established a routine.

On one occasion Greg asked to be put in a "growth group"—one of Hinson's small fellowship and accountability groups. The only one available at that time, however, met on one of his work nights. He asked for another option but was never contacted.

Greg wanted more time with me. "I really felt that I was worth salvaging, but I wasn't sure that you or others felt the same way," he said.

Later I would come to realize that Greg was a "cast sheep" during those days of discipline. That was a term I came to appreciate a number of years ago when Martha and I lived in the country. Sheep grazed near our home and we enjoyed them immensely. Each morning we would go to the window, first thing, and check on their well-being.

Early one morning I noticed one lying near the fence on its back with all four legs extended straight upward. I walked over to it, gently nudged it with my foot, and perceived no signs of life whatever. I called the owner and said, "Mr. Harlow, one of your sheep has died." He said he would be right over and hung up the telephone.

Within a few minutes he drove his truck up to the sheep, hopped out, walked over, and spent considerable time kneeling over what appeared to be a lifeless animal. He then stood up and called to me. "Don, come here; I want to show you something."

"This sheep is not dead," he said. "This is what is known as a cast sheep. Every so often a sheep that is heavy with wool or heavy with lamb will lie down, roll into a slight recess in the ground onto its back, and will find itself unable to get up. When that happens the sheep is cast or helpless. There is no possible way that a sheep can survive that position for very long. The gases begin to ruminate in its belly, the joints stiffen and atrophy, and if it's left to itself, it will die."

I watched him as he gently rolled that sheep onto its side and began massaging its limbs and body. After a brief time the legs began to relax and occasional muscle twitches seemed to confirm the fact that it was alive. It wasn't long before that gentle shepherd placed his hands under the belly of that sheep, lifted it onto its wobbly legs, and began slowly walking it until it was able to stand by itself.

Oftentimes I'll use that story to describe the condition of the many "hurting people" that are to be found in a church this size. I'll ask the staff if they know of any "cast sheep" and then we'll pray for them and devise other ways to be of encouragement.

Greg was a "cast sheep"—down—dying—and unable to get up by himself. He said, as we evaluated the period of time spent under discipline, "I had heard a lot about 'cast sheep' and I was one, but I really didn't sense a high level of concern from the staff."

"In fact," he said, "I *craved* contact with the staff. These were my closest friends—my associates. These were the ones to whom I should have been accountable, but they were not available to me. I wanted to reach out to them, but I was too ashamed and I didn't feel that I could handle any more rejection. The members of the staff were all gracious, and they were kind . . . but they remained distant. I needed them desperately."

A group of five men invited Greg to join them each week for breakfast. This quickly became the supportive fellowship that met many of Greg's needs.

They accepted him completely. They treated him as a human being and as an equal. There was no condemnation, no criticism. No conditions were imposed upon their continuing relationship. They had breakfast together, shared needs with each other, and prayed.

They studied a number of books together: *The Fight;*[1] *How to Say No to a Stubborn Habit;*[2] *Knowing God;*[3] *The Pursuit of Holiness,*[4] and others.

Each week they would read a prescribed chapter and discuss it together. Greg has repeated time and again that this was one of his major areas of support.

We seldom prayed for him publicly—which is something we should have done. I'm sure all of us prayed privately, but corporate discipline requires corporate prayer. Whether it was forgetfulness or clumsiness or simply our reluctance to keep this scar in front of the people, I don't know—but we should have prayed more as a church family. Specific prayer makes it possible to accurately measure God's responses, and since the experience of discipline was given low prayer visibility, the level of joyous response to God's continuing involvement was also low.

One friend suggested that Greg and Joanna develop a "Promise Book." She told them to write down every meaningful promise they encountered as they read the Scriptures. Then in their low times they wouldn't be forced to search their Bibles for

---

1. John White, *The Fight* (Downers Grove, Ill.: InterVarsity Press, 1976).
2. Erwin W. Lutzer, *How to Say No to a Stubborn Habit* (Wheaton: Scripture Press, 1979).
3. J. I. Packer, *Knowing God* (Downers Grove, Ill.: InterVarsity Press, 1973).
4. Jerry Bridges, *The Pursuit of Holiness* (Colorado Springs: NavPress, 1978).

help, but would already have quick access to some meaningful verses.

What helpful counsel this proved to be! At times Greg would come home after a terribly frustrating day at work, too defeated to continue. He would pick up the promise book and gain immediate strength.

They would also record specific prayer requests along with the answers to prayer. This God would often use to bolster their faith when they were tempted to feel He had deserted them.

Some of Joanna's Sunday school class members took her to an occasional lunch. Many of them wrote to her with words of encouragement.

One note contained the words from Isaiah 43:2:

"When you pass through the waters, I will be with
    you;
And through the rivers, they will not overflow you.
When you walk through the fire, you will not be
    scorched,
Nor will the flame burn you."

Greg and Joanna lived daily in this promise.

When we recommended a period of discipline for the purpose of restoration, we failed to place any time limits. In fact, we were reluctant to even suggest that complete restoration to a gospel ministry was even a remote possibility. We developed a wait-and-see attitude toward any future involvement.

One of our reasons for this reluctance was a pessimistic report from Greg's psychologist about the prospect of complete recovery. In an early meeting with the staff and board, we asked the counselor, "What are the prospects for complete recovery for a man who has been immorally involved with so many for so long?"

"The prospect is very poor," he replied. "It's seldom that one ever is able to be completely freed from this sort of life style when it has been allowed to become so ingrained in his being."

And yet, Greg did need some hope. Ministry was his life, his love, his great obsession, and the possibility that he might never be allowed to return was devastating to him. We should have been more responsive to his need for hope—but then, we kept telling ourselves, we were inexperienced and had never been down this road before.

Greg's and Joanna's continuing presence at Hinson posed other problems to both them and us.

There was constant pressure to restore Greg to his position of pastoral leadership. I was continually being called into account with questions that I was not at liberty to answer.

"Why is the process taking so long?"

"Why don't you really forgive him?"

"Is it really restoration if we fail to restore him to his place of ministry?"

There were times when I truly despaired because of the intense pressure that was brought to bear during these two years. I actually found myself hoping—and even praying on one occasion—that Greg and Joanna would leave and go somewhere else.

Many people felt embarrassed in this couple's presence. Many said, "I always feel awkward around Greg. I don't know how to act or what to say."

Some would see Greg and say, "I sure wish he would go someplace else. He ought to be ashamed to come to church here." If only they had known just how ashamed he was.

Some expressed sheer disgust, betrayal, and didn't want to even look at him. Most people were agreed that Greg should have stayed . . . but really didn't want him to.

There were those who lived in a state of shocked disbelief. They found it difficult to understand how one could display such maturity, speak with such sensitivity, pray with such power, and serve with such fervor, and yet be such a "scoundrel."

Most people were very guarded in their statements. There were few adamant feelings expressed. The overwhelming sensation was one of bewilderment—deep sorrow and loss. These feelings were combined with a constraining love to recover as much for God as possible.

As long as Greg remained here we all were forced to grapple with all of these conflicting emotions.

None of us felt truly comfortable with Greg and Joanna, and they didn't feel comfortable with us. None of us really knew what to talk about in their presence. Only a very few of us ever addressed the great heartache that persisted to cause deep and unbearable pain to this dear couple.

Greg and Joanna suffered the most. Greg developed a severe case of colitis and every time they would get up to prepare to come to church, Greg would get sick. As they approached the building, their apprehension grew. They felt overwhelmed by their shame and their dread.

Some would greet them warmly. Some would greet them coldly. Others would simply turn away. In his terribly sensitive state, Greg felt rejection from almost everyone, but later concluded that it was not rejection nearly so much as it was simple clumsiness from people who didn't know what to say.

They sat together in the back of the left-hand side of the auditorium every Sunday. It seemed strange to see Greg sitting with Joanna in church. This was a privilege they had often longed for, but didn't expect to happen.

Greg's head was usually bowed. I was seldom able to make eye contact with him. I often wondered what he was thinking. Was he even listening? *Could* he listen? Or was he so consumed by his embarrassment that he was unable to concentrate on anything but himself?

He told me later that all of the above were true at first. Before long he developed a hunger for the Bible that caused him to hang on every word. He couldn't get enough. We were studying the Book of Hebrews, and he claimed that it was tremendously helpful to him.

He also listened to cassette tapes and sermons. The radio ministry of Charles Swindoll was a great source of help, as he and Joanna tuned him in every morning.

But still . . . the deep emotional responses to exposure and humiliation prevailed and kept all of us uncomfortable for months. This was a heavy price to pay for the restoration of one brother, it seemed, because it cast a pall over the entire church that always seemed to diminish our excitement. It caused us to feel "on guard" and restrained. Uncomfortable.

But it was worth it.

I will never forget the Sunday, six months after the humiliation, when Greg sat in a new Sunday morning seat, halfway down toward the front, head erect, eyes glowing, and with a look of expectancy on his face. At some point in the sermon I said something that touched him deeply. I saw his head bob up and down and heard a hearty "amen."

Greg's back, I thought. From that moment it seemed that we all began to relax and enjoy each other again.

CHAPTER TEN

Forgiveness and Restoration

Joanna's response was crucial to Greg on that fateful Thursday when his world came crashing in on him. After each confrontation he would slip away, call his wife, and tell her he loved her. She didn't know the truth yet—and wouldn't until that evening.

Looking back on that black day, Joanna said that it was the unexpected phone calls—that repeated "I love you"—that seemed real to her. In the car, as Greg confessed his infidelity and sobbed out his desire for forgiveness—*that* seemed unreal. Impossible. A crazy, unbelievable nightmare that would end—had to end—soon.

And yet it did not end. It just kept building.

"I was actually in a state of shock," she recalled. "Much like the shock that temporarily blocks out physical pain, I experienced an emotional shock that caused me to feel nothing, but rather seemed to wrap me completely in a state of emotional numbness.

"As the numbness began to wear off, I felt a great pity for Greg's bitter anguish, and yet it was not only pity—there were genuine feelings of love and tenderness as he could barely speak between racking sobs that convulsed his whole body.

"There were times when I felt more like a mother than a wife. I so wanted to help him and to comfort him through his terrible pain.

"My big, strong, decisive husband was suddenly as weak and helpless as a child. Soon my children would be devastated, too, and I began to realize that the tremendous, almost impossible task of helping them all through this horrible grief and disillusionment was to rest squarely and solely upon me.

"Our children adored their daddy and his approval was so important to all of them. 'Your daddy will be so proud of you' was an important phrase at our house. Their admiration was so great—I knew their pain would be acute.

"I was so overwhelmed with my responsibility to Greg and my children during those first few shattering moments that I really forgot to feel how this whole nightmare was affecting me."

During the hours and days that followed, Joanna's emotional anaesthetic wore off. She experienced great anger, bitterness, and self-pity. Various incidents would come to mind that had always been remembered as wonderful and happy times with many of her close friends. As she recalled them carefully she would realize that those happy occasions had often been used by her husband and her friends as opportunities for infidelity. Her contented past seemed to be more and more obscured with an ugly awareness that she had been deceived, betrayed, cheated, and wronged. The past thirteen years blurred into one long nightmare as she saw Greg and his sin in every memory. She found herself turning even the most innocent events into ugly experiences—until finally there were no longer any happy memories.

As her struggles increased, so did Greg's. He was constantly depressed and Joanna found herself torn between trying to fight the immense battles going on within her and at the same time trying to encourage her husband in his struggles.

She never seriously considered leaving her husband—she realized quickly that the only real biblical option that she had was to forgive him.

From childhood she had been trained in forgiveness. One of her earliest memories was that of learning Ephesians 4:32:

> And be kind to one another, tender-hearted, forgiving each other, just as God in Christ also has forgiven you.

Her parents would quote that verse to the children whenever there was any kind of quarrel. She knew it well—it had been so deeply etched in her heart and mind that any other response to her husband's sin seemed out of the question. As she considered her responses, every Scripture verse she had ever learned about forgiveness flooded back into her memory. Sometimes they were just phrases; at other times, they were great chunks of Scripture—all of them confirming her one responsibility—to stay with the husband of her youth and genuinely and totally forgive him.

"Beside that," she said, "we loved each other. We had always spent large amounts of time together. We resented being apart even when Greg would leave home for one of his many conferences. Greg would very often call from the church and say, 'Let's go for a ride,' or 'Let's have lunch.' All of our hobbies, skiing, hiking, camping, were hobbies we could do together. We were a close family and we loved each other. Greg and I never slept well unless we could cuddle.

"I've always believed that we Christians are to forgive as we have been forgiven. Forgiveness is not just a good suggestion or a helpful idea. God commands it. Of course I would forgive as my husband had asked. Forgiveness was the normal response even in this totally abnormal situation, and my forgiveness would have to be total and complete, unless I wanted something less than my Heavenly Father's total and complete blessing."

Oftentimes in the middle of these musings she would hear herself saying, "Certainly I'll forgive him, but then I really won't have to, because I'll be waking up—this nightmare will end—and everything will be all right again."

Joanna had the same problem most of us in the church had: Forgiveness did not guarantee her the ability to forget. Our memories were all too sharply tuned in to recollections of that horrible confession.

Counseling was a necessity. Joanna carried deep feelings of guilt because her seeming forgiveness did not eliminate periodic bouts with quiet anger and temporary desires to withdraw—even recoil—from her husband.

I asked her, "How did you display your forgiveness to Greg?" She thought for a few moments and then began to list some steps she had taken that helped to rebuild her man's shattered life:

"I told him I loved him—repeatedly."

"I told him I forgave him—repeatedly."

"I stayed with him."

"I listened to him."
"I comforted him."
"I protected him."
"I slept with him."
"I initiated sex with him."

As I look back on all the crucial steps taken that ultimately resulted in Greg's restoration, two facts stand out: the fact that Greg and Joanna were urged to remain at Hinson to experience the love and forgiveness of the body, and the fact of Joanna's willingness to forgive her husband.

Without her strong determination to obey God there would have been no restoration.

CHAPTER ELEVEN

Submission and Restoration

Greg himself played a significant part in his own recovery. He willingly made himself subject to his church and its leadership.

I have always been acutely aware of the presence of Hebrews 13:17 in Scripture:

> Obey your leaders, and submit to them; for they keep watch over your souls, as those who will give an account. Let them do this with joy and not with grief, for this would be unprofitable for you.

It seems that there are few Scriptures people heed less than this one. Accountability is rare. So is submission to authority. Those of us who lead find it extremely difficult to require it, request it, or demand it.

Jesus began His relationship with His disciples with two words. These were a command—a command to be obeyed—a command that placed each of those twelve men in a submissive, dependent, accountable role. The words, *"Follow Me,"* meant nothing more and nothing less than just "do what you're told."

Any organization that plans any degree of success in fulfilling its role in this world must have both leaders and followers. Leaders must lead and followers must follow.

Any leader who plans to lead must give commands. Pastors dare not play their leadership role as drill sergeants in the military. We do not bark clipped demands to our people. We do not shout orders to the congregations. But we do command a following, and even though our commands are carefully couched so as not to offend or wound, they *are* commands with significant authority behind them.

When we entered into a discipline relationship with Greg, we asked him if he was willing to be completely submissive to the church in general and to the staff and board in particular. We asked him if on certain occasions he would submit to me, the pastor.

This placed me in the position of that leader described in Hebrews 13:17, who was responsible to keep watch over Greg's soul—and to give an account. There were few decisions I was forced to make without the collective wisdom of at least my staff, but there were times when I was the one required to say yes or no to many of Greg's requests.

Greg never accepted any invitation to minister in any form or to any degree without first consulting with me.

Nearly every week there was a request, and nearly every week during that first year, I was forced to say no. Greg needed time to feel the enormity of his sin. He needed time to feel the reality of forgiveness. He needed time to recover his own self-confidence. He needed time to feel comfortable with God and to learn to feel comfortable with people. Greg just needed time.

Saying no when I knew he was slowly dying on the inside for some opportunity to minister was one of the most difficult things I've ever done. I'm an old "softy" who finds it difficult to deprive anyone of anything—and to deprive Greg was terribly hard.

He would come to me, describe an invitation, make his appeal, and I would say, "No, not yet, Greg." I would then hear his beautifully obedient "All right, whatever you say" and watch the expectancy in his face drain away into disappointment. He'd never argue, but it was obvious that he wished I would throw just one yes in his direction.

I would then take that request, tuck it away in my consciousness, and mull it over and over again. *Did I make the right decision? Am I causing Greg too much sorrow? How do we know when he's had enough?* It was often necessary for me to run these requests by the staff and board to gain their perspective and make sure that I was doing the right thing.

It got to the place where I almost shunned him. There were times I didn't want to talk to him or would delay returning his phone calls or the requests from others, simply because I wanted to be spared having to speak that inevitable no. I wanted to avoid that carefully masked—but all too obvious—disappointment.

But Greg obeyed. Always. He submitted himself to us completely. He did not always appreciate our decisions, but he obeyed them.

He obeyed when we told him that we felt he should remain at Hinson until he was restored. This was the most difficult demand that we placed upon him, the one that inflicted the greatest pain, because he was constantly forced to stand in the presence of people who knew just what he had done.

But he stayed.

Gradually, one by one, we lifted the restrictions. He was allowed at first to minister in Sunday school classes and at social gatherings. Then to larger groups. Eventually he was permitted to teach one of the largest Sunday school classes in the church. The first time he was allowed back on the platform to minister in the church auditorium, he played "O love that will not let me go" and "I am loved, I am loved, I can risk loving you, for the One who knows me best, loves me most."

The restoration of the sinner was due in great part to the obedience of the sinner. Without Greg's submission, restoration would have been impossible.

CHAPTER TWELVE

Chastening and Restoration

Greg suffered deeply for his sin.

For thirteen years he had been "looking over his shoulder"—furtively watching in all directions for the discovery that he knew some day would take place. For thirteen years he looked in a mirror and saw a phony. For thirteen years he was forced to invent lies and to deceive the one person he most wanted to trust him—his wife. For thirteen years he lived with the mental images of numerous experiences of infidelity that would fleetingly and unexpectedly cross before his eyes even in the most holy and sacred moments. For thirteen years he tried to imagine what it would be like to be pure and clean and honest and real, but these qualities had long since left him. For thirteen years he looked at his children and wondered which ones would turn out to be like him and how that could be prevented. He wondered what they would say when they discovered the truth about their dad. For thirteen years he was forced to shift emotional gears repeatedly from loving his wife to loving his many partners in sin. For thirteen years he tried to study the Scriptures and pray, but the pages would blur and the words refuse to come.

Thirteen years of emotional chaos, of spiritual deadness. Thirteen years of abject fear.

One would think that this, in itself, would be sufficient suffering for sin. For many it has been. Some collapse under the heavy load of guilt. The sensitized conscience of the believer never ceases to function. It may grow hardened and calloused, it may even be seared,[1] but it still continues to speak. The conscience begins whispering to us as a friend before it finally screams to us as a judge.

Some die. Feelings of guilt can be deadly and can cause depression and other forms of minor and major illness. Suicide is common among those who have sacrificed a lifetime of principle for a few moments of pleasure.

David, the psalmist, described the relentless pain of unforgiven sin in Psalm 32. He wrote:

When I kept silent about my sin, my body wasted
  away
Through my groaning all day long.

For day and night Thy hand was heavy upon me;
My vitality was drained away as with the fever heat of
  summer.

I acknowledged my sin to Thee,
And my iniquity I did not hide;
I said, "I will confess my transgressions to the LORD";
And Thou didst forgive the guilt of my sin (vv. 3-5).

He suggested that his body no longer served him—its strength was dissipated, and he was limited by continued weakness.

His spirit groaned, and often those groans would pass unexpectedly through his lips and fall—with bewildering intensity—on the ears of those listening.

He was in bondage to his sin, his body, and even his God as the heavy constraining hand of the Almighty restricted him from the spiritual and physical freedom he had always enjoyed. He was imprisoned by his guilt.

The lines of communication had been cut. There were no longer any joyous feelings of sacred interchange between this man and his God. David and God seemed separated by infinity, and the psalmist had not only lost all feelings of divine access, but also all sense of divine resource. He said that the cumulative

---

1. 1 Timothy 4:2

weaknesses of sin had finally taken their toll. He felt drained of all energy and vitality as though he had just been forced to endure the oppressive heat and stifling humidity of an unbearably hot summer day.

Like David, Greg suffered far more than just the fear of exposure and the pain of guilt and hypocrisy. God's chastening is always sure and inevitable.

> . . . and you have forgotten the exhortation which is addressed to you as sons, "My son, do not regard lightly the discipline of the Lord, nor faint when you are reproved by Him . . ." (Hebrews 12:5).

It is always important that the believer learn to distinguish between divine punishment and divine chastisement.

As problems increased in Greg's life, many would ask, "Greg, is God punishing you?" To this he would always answer, "No." Greg had lost much, but he never let go of his theological precision. The Scriptures were exacting on this point, and he was always able to delineate between punishment and chastisement.

God's people can *never* be punished for their sins. The believer's sins have already been punished on the cross. Jesus suffered the full penalty for sin, and by His shed blood we have been cleansed.[2]

Jesus canceled all our debts on the cross and marked them "paid in full" so that no child of God need fear judgment for any sin.

> . . . having canceled out the certificate of debt consisting of decrees against us and which was hostile to us; and He has taken it out of the way, having nailed it to the cross (Colossians 2:14).

As a result, there is therefore now no condemnation (or judgment) for those who are in Christ Jesus.[3] God cannot exact payment for what Christ has already paid in full.

God's children must and do experience chastisement, however. Chastisement is the necessary and inevitable child training process that, in its extreme, can take on the form of "scourg-

---

2. 1 John 1:9
3. Romans 8:1

84   Chastening and Restoration

ings"[4]—physical pain—or can come as gentle, mild, whispered reminders of God's wishes to the minds of His children.

Chastisement can be corrective and it can be preventative.

Job's chastisement was for the purpose of revealing Jehovah God to the world, God to Job, and Job to himself.[5]

Abraham's chastisement was simply for the development of spiritual graces in his life.

Paul was chastised, not for his sin, but to prevent him from becoming proud.[6]

David experienced the severe blows of God's chastening rod for his open wickedness.[7]

Chastening is designed for perfecting.

For they disciplined us for a short time as seemed best to them, but He disciplines us for our good, that we may share His holiness. All discipline for the moment seems not to be joyful, but sorrowful; yet to those who have been trained by it, afterwards it yields the peaceful fruit of righteousness (Hebrews 12:10-11).

Greg's chastening began with the whispered warnings that pled with him before he fell. They continued to grow in intensity as he persisted. Chastening came in full force with his exposure, continued through his humiliation, and is still in effect today as he battles with a tortured memory and a smeared reputation.

The one great fear in the apostle Paul's life was that he would lose his self-control to the point of being disqualified for gospel ministry:

. . . but I buffet my body and make it my slave, lest possibly, after I have preached to others, I myself should be disqualified (1 Corinthians 9:27).

Greg was disqualified—placed on the shelf—no longer privileged to serve.

I asked him on one occasion, "How do you feel about being forced out of the ministry?"

---

4. Hebrews 12:6
5. Job 42:5-6
6. 2 Corinthians 12:7
7. 2 Samuel 12:10-14

"Worthless, unworthy, useless," he answered. "There are times when I want nothing more than to die—I pray to die. I'm not suicidal, I'm too big a coward for that, but often I ask God to take me home."

He was no longer a minister; he was no longer employed. The church gave him one month's salary beyond his termination date, but those thirty days flew by like the wind. He was soon brought face to face with the stark reality of being a provider with no income. Like many of us he had no reserves, no savings, no resources other than his regular paycheck.

He prayed for a job—he asked for an income—but of even greater importance he prayed that he might be a man after God's own heart. He turned off his television set—permanently—closed his magazines, his newspapers, all extraneous reading material, and immersed himself in the Scriptures. He allowed nothing to be set before his eyes that could distract him or remind him. He refused to be diverted from his goal to experience the full approval of God and the full respect of his family.

God allowed chastening to continue. Satan used every tactic imaginable to frustrate him from reaching his goal.

At first he couldn't find work. When he finally did, he soon discovered that he was not cut out to be a telephone salesman. His first month on the job he earned $38. He was a total failure.

Some fellow church members brought him into their insurance agency. But he hated the insurance business. He faced each day with dread and entered into it only by sheer determination. He forced himself to make appointments and to call on prospects.

The first month was a good one—even a promising one. He surprised himself and his associates. But it was all downhill from there. When he finally quit, twenty-five months later, his average income was $100 per week.

Upon arriving in Portland, Greg and Joanna had purchased their dream home: spacious, comfortable, and with a magnificent view of the Columbia River and the mountains to the north. The purchase required most of their equity from a previous sale, and the payments were higher than they could afford, but they reasoned that others would live with them and share costs.

Greg and Joanna struggled vainly to keep their home. Many times the church would make their house payment for them, but finally they ran out of options and resources, and they lost their home. With the loss of the house went more than $30,000 in equity that would never be recovered. When Greg's restoration was complete and they finally left Hinson, they had less than $700 of their own money and $850 given them as a love offering from the members of their Sunday school class.

Greg looked constantly for other jobs, but each time it seemed to him that God shut the door.

They talked seriously about moving. Although Greg had agreed to stay at Hinson, he argued that if he was going to be miserable, they might as well at least move someplace where they could be miserable less miserably.

Joanna, who had always been the picture of health, had four major surgeries for cancer in thirteen months. We never mentioned it when I visited with her in the hospital or when I talked with Greg . . . but all three of us wondered what relationship possibly existed between Joanna's illness and Greg's sin.

Oftentimes I would see the abject despair in Greg's eyes as he wondered what possible calamity could happen next.

There was more. Two of the children in a distant state suffered through a long series of earthquakes where many of their personal possessions were destroyed and their families' lives were threatened. Visiting their children, Greg and Joanna survived four major earthquakes in one night.

All of the family members experienced major traumatic experiences during that twenty-six month period of discipline and restoration.

On one occasion Greg was convinced that he could work his way into a church near his home—a church that needed talents and had already made overtures to discuss a future ministry with him.

He asked me for permission, and I refused.

He asked Joanna, and she also agreed that it would be an act of rebellion and could jeopardize his healing.

Greg became angry and was about to move out from under the umbrella of accountability when Joanna—suddenly and for the first time—displayed intense anger toward her husband. She refused to allow him to even consider such an option. He submitted and gave his future back to the Lord and to us—his church. We felt so helpless at that time. Oh, how we wanted to play God in Greg's life and remove him from his suffering and restore him before the time was right.

Greg, however, was convinced through it all that he was *not* being punished. He was being chastened and occasionally being tested to see if his desire to fully please God was totally genuine.

Even in his time of great impatience, he held onto the promise of Hebrews 12:11:

> All discipline for the moment seems not to be joyful, but sorrowful; yet to those who have been trained by it, afterwards it yields the peaceful fruit of righteousness.

Afterwards—after it's all over—it yields righteousness. And peace.

This was the hope to which he clung.

CHAPTER THIRTEEN

Set Apart to Serve—Again

Greg's reordination was a celebration. It came just fifty-five weeks following the advent of his discipline. We had not acknowledged any specific plans to take steps toward restoration at the end of that year, but we had determined to thoroughly review the discipline process and to at least consider some positive recommendation regarding Greg's future.

The first encouragement came in the form of a letter from his counselor, a psychologist within our body, addressed to the chairman of the Board of Deacons.

> Mr. Chuck Marvin, Chairman
> Board of Deacons
> Hinson Memorial Baptist Church
>
> I have worked with Greg this year on a weekly basis, professionally. Greg has responded well to the counseling. He has looked at himself both psychologically and biblically and seems to have good understanding of many of the bases of the problem that we have been concerned about.
>
> He demonstrates warmth and fervor in loving God. He has been willing for God to bring anything into

his life, however severe it may be, in order to bring restoration.

He deeply longs for ministry again. He is also constantly guarding areas of his life through which temptation may again occur.

It is my considered opinion that it would be of particular advantage to Greg if he were to begin afresh in a church other than Hinson.

I would strongly urge you to consider this brother for full restoration and placement in the ministry again.

This encouraging recommendation was in sharp contrast to the rather pessimistic outlook this counselor had given more than nine months earlier.

The counseling sessions had been very productive. Greg had been helped to see how he had been viewing women as objects rather than persons. He was given insight into the mechanics of seduction and how these immoral relationships develop. In addition, the counselor had given Greg two things he desperately needed: hope and acceptance.

In a meeting with Greg and Joanna following the receipt of the counselor's letter, we listened carefully to the reports of progress that had already begun to appear to anyone who was looking for them. It was obvious that the feelings of guilt had begun to diminish. The heaviness had been lifted. The oppressive shame was no longer evident. Greg and Joanna mingled freely as they came to the services on Sunday. The clumsiness that many had felt earlier seemed to be gone.

As the staff met with Greg and Joanna, we asked some probing questions about their recovery.

To Joanna we asked, "What is happening in Greg's life that seems to assure that you'll never be forced to go through the shameful experience again?"

She was radiant. "My husband is a changed man," she said. "He has become the spiritual leader that I had always hoped he would be. He prays for me and with me. His prayers are prayers of depth and meaning. He leads us in family devotions each morning at the breakfast table. He is displaying a love for God and an appreciation for me that I have craved for more than twenty-eight years."

Since most of the immoral relationships had developed in counseling sessions, we were quite concerned that he be carefully guarded in this area.

Greg and Joanna had already made some significant decisions in this area.

Greg would never counsel a woman alone more than once.

He would then either refer her to another or he would enter into a team counseling relationship. He would use Joanna as much as possible. In fact, one safeguard that they hoped might become reality was the possibility that Joanna might assume a position alongside him.

We asked Greg, "How are you going to keep these memories fresh so that you'll not fall back into sin?"

With that he showed me a plaque and a key ring, both bearing the name of the insurance company for which he worked. "One will hang on my wall and the other I'll keep in my pocket to remind me of the most miserable months of my life," he said.

We recommended that his ordination be restored to him.

The service was much like any other ordination service, except that the spirit of that meeting was vastly different.

I felt deeply grateful to God as I prayed. Many of the men gathered in that expanded circle around Greg wept openly as they placed their hands on his head. We were fully aware that something unique and something wonderful was happening.

As communion was served, the staff took the elements first to Greg and Joanna. We counted it a high honor to serve them.

Following the reordination service, Greg wrote the following to me:

Dear Pastor,

We've often wanted to thank you for the way in which you've borne the grief and pain my sin caused you and the Hinson family. The extra pressures this brought on you and the staff are part of the ache in my heart that memory calls forth again and again.

Thank you for showing spiritual courage in asking us to stay this past year. It would have been so much easier for you and the church if we had simply limped away. But no restoration could then have occurred— no chance to glorify God through public forgiveness and restoration of one publicly shamed.

Thank you again for being willing to be used in my discipline and healing. Any future ministry God may allow us will surely be due to your courage and the backing of the staff and deacon board.

Joanna and I pray regularly for you and all who exercise godly authority at Hinson. Surely God's blessing is on you all.

In Christ,

Greg

In reordaining Greg, we had commended him to God for whatever ministry God would feel appropriate. We had commended him to *the* ministry, not *a* ministry. He was still without a job.

Many were disappointed that we had not invited him to rejoin the Hinson staff. There were, however, a number of reasons for this. We already had a very capable replacement. And there were those in the church that felt strongly against asking Greg to rejoin the staff. His counselor, too, had recommended that he start fresh somewhere else.

As the weeks and months dragged on, I became anxious and perplexed. The longer Greg went without a place to minister, the greater the pressure on me to invite him to work at Hinson. Many suggested that the restoration would be incomplete until we did. I often struggled with that possibility.

For Greg, the hope of returning to ministry gave way to fear as the months passed. He was becoming increasingly convinced that God was through with him—that he would never again return to full-time ministry.

He was failing as an insurance salesman. They had lost their home and were being faced with the question of how and where to store their furniture. Ministry was no longer merely an urgent desire—it was now survival!

Where can we go? What can I do? In some respects the anxiety was even greater during that second year of waiting. In other respects, however, it was the most profitable learning time. It gave Greg time to recover some of his shattered self-confidence. It gave him opportunities to experience the support of many Christian friends, and it also helped him realize how much he had really given up when he traded his purity for indulgent pleasure. The terribly high price of sin came into even sharper focus during that second year than it had in the first.

I longed to help Greg in any way I could. More than once I tried to hurry God in the process. Wherever I would hear of staff openings, I would call the pastor or chairman of the board and recommend Greg to them. Most of the churches in our area knew about Greg, had heard of his restoration, and didn't seem frightened of him in the least. Yet nothing ever came of my contacts.

I was aware of Greg's restlessness and fear, and as soon as I would hear of an opening, I'd call him and would sense a temporary lift of his spirit only to watch it sag back into disappointment.

Hinson, however, allowed him almost limitless opportunities for service that second year. And wherever Greg ministered, God blessed. It was obvious to us that God was not through with him. But our continuing question remained.

"What's God waiting for?"

CHAPTER FOURTEEN

Restored!

The silence of my study was interrupted by the persistent ring of the telephone. A longtime friend from a distant city was calling.

"I'm sorry, Don, to interrupt your morning, but I'm interested in one of your people. We desperately need a staff man here, and it seems that from what I've heard, your man Greg meets the qualifications for the job."

I listened as he described their church and their needs. Then I asked the question that had to be asked—the last question in the world that I wanted to ask.

"Do you know that Greg has been under discipline here at Hinson for the past twenty-six months?"

"Yes," he answered.

"Do you know why?" I asked.

"I'm not sure I know the whole story, but I understand there was some moral problem in his past."

I then proceeded to tell him the entire story—all that I knew—in confidence. I have always been a firm believer in the necessity for correct information to be passed from church to church regarding prospective staff people.

When I finished there was a long pause, and then the question for which I had waited so long: "Do you think he is ready to go back to work?"

"Absolutely!" I answered. "He has undergone his discipline admirably. He has completed nine months of psychological counseling. He has proven his repentance and has completely forsaken his sin. He has assumed the spiritual leadership of his home and family. His and Joanna's relationship is stronger than it has ever been. He is displaying himself as a man of God. In fact, I think Greg is probably better equipped to serve Christ today than most of us who have never been through the terribly painful process of discipline and restoration."

It wasn't long before Greg received his "call" back to the ministry. He accepted with great enthusiasm.

The church was smaller than any he had ever served. The salary was barely adequate, but those things were incidental to the fact that Greg was being offered a second chance. He could hardly wait to accept it.

The night of their farewell finally came—twenty-six months and two weeks from the night of their humiliation. The church family crowded back into the same auditorium to face the same two people. This time, however, it was not with shame. It was with great joy.

I invited Greg and Joanna to the platform and said, "I think everybody knows, without having to review past experiences, what's been happening with Greg and Joanna. For twenty-six months we have undergone a very painful discipline experience with Greg. When Greg fell in battle, we regarded him as a wounded soldier. We rushed to his aid and attempted to help him up. He responded beautifully. He let us help him. We loved him, and we watched him as he responded to the grace of God and the love of the church family in a way that I've never seen demonstrated before. For two years and two months we have watched the Spirit of God at work in him and through him and in us and through us, restoring a man to active ministry.

"We asked ourselves when it all began, 'Is it possible?' We asked Greg, 'Are you willing to stay right here in the body and let us love you back into the ministry?' The hardest and most crucial decision that Greg and Joanna made was that one. 'Yes,' he answered. I watched Greg week after week as he came into this building. It was painful for him to walk among his friends. We were all fully aware of the pain that was in his heart. But it was here, in his obedience and in our presence, that his healing took place. Now the healing is complete.

"Greg and Joanna are different people. They were great people when they came. Today they are among the greatest I know. I want to thank them publicly for the way they have submitted themselves to God and to the church. I don't know that I've ever experienced such willing submission—and such painful—as I have seen in them."

I then drew them to me, arms around them both, and said, "Greg and Joanna, I want to thank you for the way you've allowed God to work in your lives. I want to thank you for being responsive to the Holy Spirit. God has possibly made you better qualified to minister today than anybody I know.

"That was what I told the pastor of the church that called you, and I do believe it. Greg knows more of the dangers of life and the ministry today than those of us who have never experienced such discipline. Again, we want to say, 'Thank you.' "

I then turned to Greg and said, "Is there anything you'd like to say to the church family tonight?"

Greg's appearance and demeanor in the pulpit were vastly different from the night he acknowledged his sin. He stood erect, shoulders thrown back, head raised, and eyes scanning every upturned face.

"What Pastor and the staff and the board did," said Greg, "took guts. I don't know of any church that has behaved in this manner toward one who has fallen. At least, I've never heard of it being done. It took courage to be the first, and I think God has honored that. He has certainly honored it in our lives because we're not the same people we were. We're quite different, thank the Lord. And we know from some of you that it's had an effect on your lives as well. You have shared that with us, and we are really grateful. Thank you, Pastor, for having the courage to invite us to stay, because that's the only reason we did. It would have been far easier to walk out and never see you again, believe me.

"And there were some others who helped, too. There was the man who counseled me for nine months, and there were five guys that I met with every Thursday morning for two years, who were very supportive of me, and I really appreciated that.

"Our Sunday school class has been very supportive. We sat

in that class for a year, Sunday after Sunday, and they just gathered around and loved us. What a unique experience! It was a very precious time. They asked me to teach them, and through that teaching many shared with us and helped us and caused us to grow.

"And I would also like to thank my family, because therein lies the real nitty-gritty of this whole experience. If you have ever wanted to know a godly woman, here's one." Greg drew Joanna to him as he honored her publicly for her significant part in his restoration. The entire church responded with spontaneous applause.

"Our children were behind us one hundred percent and were supportive the whole time, and God has just really blessed us as a family. In fact, all our relatives supported us without any reservation whatever.

"I'll tell you, it is really rich when you're obedient. I want to say again to any of you who are messing around in sin, let it go, give it up, ask God for forgiveness, and come back to the fold because therein lies true blessing and joy and peace.

"And then above all, I would thank God for His restorative power to make a new man of me and to allow me again the privilege of being a minister. What a glorious God we have."

With those words we concluded twenty-six of the most difficult and yet most instructive months in the life of our church family. Months of pain and perfecting. Months devoted to salvaging a worthy servant and restoring him to productive ministry.

As Martha and I went home that night, the weariness was good, and the need for approval was only slight. We didn't ask whether or not we had done the right thing or said the right thing. We simply relaxed—relaxed with the realization that maybe— just maybe—we had finally done it right.

We forgave a fallen brother. But we didn't stop there. Cooperating with God, we moved beyond forgiveness, restoring a sinning saint to a life of meaning and ministry.

Bibliography

Hay, Alex Rattray. *The New Testament Order for Church and Missionary.* Audobon, N.J.: New Testament Missionary Union, 1947.

Saucy, Robert L. *The Church in God's Program.* Chicago: Moody Press, 1972.

Schaeffer, Francis A. *The Church Before the Watching World.* Downers Grove, Ill.: InterVarsity Press, 1971.

Walker, Warham. *Harmony in the Church: Church Discipline.* Rochester, N.Y.: Backus Book Publishers, 1844. (1981 Reprint).

Wray, Daniel E. *Biblical Church Discipline.* Carlisle, Pa.: The Banner of Truth Trust, 1978.

Scripture Index

Exodus
20:14 36

Deuteronomy
19:15 39

Joshua
7:1-26 35

2 Samuel
12:10-14 84

Job
42:5-6 84

Psalms
32:3-5 82

Isaiah
43:2 69

Matthew
18 . . . . 38, 48
18:14 49
18:15-20 . . . . 33, 35
18:15 . . . . . 34, 36, 38, 39
18:16 . . . . 39, 40
18:17 . . . . 40, 41
18:18-20 42
18:20 40
18:21-22 41

Mark
2:14 77
10:1-9 36

Luke
9:52-56 41
15 62
15:10 62

John
8:1-11 18
17:21, 23 45

Acts
5:1-11 33

Romans
8:1 83
14:1 44
16:17 45

1 Corinthians
5 55
5:1-5 33
5:1 . . . . 55, 56
5:2 56
5:3-4 56
5:5 . . . . . 34, 42, 56, 58
5:6 56
5:7 56
5:6-8 34
5:10-11 36
5:11 . . . . 30, 45
6:1-5 40
9:27 84
11:27-30 58
11:31 29
11:32 58

2 Corinthians
2 58
2:1-11 58
2:6-7 58
2:7 . . . . 48, 49
2:8 34
12:7 84

Galatians
5:12 44
6:1 . . . . 34, 35

Ephesians
4:2 41
4:11-12 47
4:15 37
4:32 74

Philippians
1:9-10 9

Colossians
2:14 83
2:16 44

1 Thessalonians
4:8 36
5:14 33

2 Thessalonians
3:6-15 33
3:15 . . . . 35, 50

1 Timothy
1:20 44
3:2 . . . . 46, 47, 49
3:3 46
3:4 46
3:6 . . . . 47, 48
3:7 47
4:2 82
4:14 47
5:17 47

5:17-22 57
5:19 . . . . 39, 57
5:20 . . . . 34, 35, 50, 57

2 Timothy
1:13, 14 47
2:17 44
2:24 . . . . 46, 47
2:24-25 46
2:24-26 47
4:5 47

Titus
1:6 . . . . 46, 47
1:7 . . . . 46, 47
1:6-7 . . . . . . 46, 47, 49
1:8 . . . . 46, 47
1:9 47
1:13 34
3:10 34

Hebrews
6 . . . . 51, 55
6:1-6 52
12:5 83
12:6 . . . . 46, 84
12:10-11 84
12:11 87
13:17 . . . . 77, 78

1 Peter
1:16 10
5:2-3 47

2 Peter
3:9 41

1 John
1:9 . . . . 29, 83
4:1, 2, 3 44

Revelation
2:14-15 44
2, 3 34